The World's Daftest Rabbit
& other stories

Illustrations by Amanda Dixon
Published in Great Britain by D C Thomson & Co. Ltd.,
185 Fleet Street, London EC4A 2HS.
www.dcthomson.co.uk

The Daftest Rabbit In The World

Welcome to the first ever collection of Chris Pascoe's Fun Tales columns from My Weekly magazine. Join Ted the rabbit, surely the world's daftest, as he stumbles through life, falling asleep in his food, failing to grasp the simplest of concepts, such as sleeping in his sleeping compartment and at the mercy of his far-more-intelligent and occasionally feisty, partner Billie.

CONTENTS

The Daftest Rabbit In The World

Chris Pascoe Collection

Chris's Animal Magic

Meet The Author

Fancy That

A DANGER TO HIMSELF

An erratic rabbit provides the latest challenge for our intrepid sitter...

Recently I mentioned that I thought I may own the world's dumbest rabbit. After much reflection, I unreservedly withdraw this statement – Ted is definitely the world's dumbest rabbit.

There's nothing wrong with sitting around all day chewing hay and staring at a wall; indeed, that pretty much describes my own day. But does he really need to be so alarmed by said wall that he will suddenly fly into the air and back-flip into his food bowl?

I look after a few rabbits on my pet-sitting rounds, and not one of the others seem to feel the need to perform aerial gymnastics into their own dinner.

Mind you, one of these, a rabbit named Boris, seems to have fallen head over giant back paws in love with a Burmese cat. The cat will climb into the rabbit's hutch and the two will curl up happily together for hours. Sweet and cute, but also very dangerous – always best to keep an eye on that pairing!

Ted can better that; he's fallen in love with a toy cat which he'll spend hours grooming, before becoming annoyed at the lack of reciprocal care and back-kicking it in the face. Not the brightest candle in the church, our Ted.

It all came to a head when we purchased a new hutch for Ted last month. He's a spoilt rabbit and has always lived in an indoors

pen, but after worriedly observing his strange love affair with the stuffed toy, we decided he was in need of a mate. With little room indoors, it had to be a spacious two-storey hutch in the garden for Ted and his bride-to-be. But there was a problem – Ted totally failed to understand the concept of steps.

After three days on the bottom level of his luxury two-storey accommodation, it became clear that Ted had no idea he had an "upstairs".

With Billie's arrival only days away, we decided we'd have to help. We couldn't let Ted have the embarrassment of admitting to his guest that he had absolutely no idea where his bedroom was.

We took Ted out of the bottom of the hutch and put him in the bed chamber of the top half. The plan was that he'd notice the gaping hole and steps leading downstairs and cautiously make his way down.

No. Within seconds, Ted shot through the bedroom arch like a

He's fallen in love with a toy cat which he'll groom for hours

bat out of hell, dropped straight through the open hole, and bowled head over heels down his ladder.

I lurched forward into the open bottom half of the hutch to help him, putting all of my considerable weight onto the hutch floor, and the floor disappeared below the hutch, as did Ted. My wife stared in astonishment. All that remained was the back end of a fat bloke disappearing into a rabbit hutch. On reflection, I now realise that Ted isn't the one I should have written about. I may well be the world's dumbest rabbit owner.

A RABBIT ROMANCE

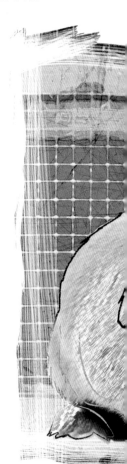

Will Chris's lonely, cognitively challenged rabbit Ted ever find a mate?...

Recently, I wrote about the world's dumbest rabbit, Ted. My very own rabbit. He proved to be only one step above me on whatever scale stupidity is measured on – as shown by my previously mentioned attempts at jumping into Ted's hutch.

We re-built the two-storey hutch after I destroyed it, and Ted finally worked out how to find his hutch-bedroom. We were now all set for the arrival of his bride-to-be. After a few glitches with his original fiancée Billie (she got housed elsewhere) we set about finding Ted a new mate. We'd seen an ad by a national rescue organisation, appealing for help with their homeless bunny crisis, and decided Ted would very much like to help them. It was here that we ran into problems.

"You say your hutch is five feet," said the volunteer. "That's not big enough."

"Not big enough? It was the biggest hutch in the pet shop.

"It's several storeys high, and the run's big too."

"No, you'll need a bigger one. Your run isn't safe either – foxes will burrow in."

"Foxes? But the rabbits will only be in the run in the daytime, right outside the window. A fox would never have time to burrow in."

"Foxes, Mr Pascoe, foxes. And your hutch is too small."

I glanced at Ted's monster hutch and wondered what sort of rabbit mansion was required. We had to give up on adopting there. Their bunny crisis is ongoing. Not at all sure why…

The next day, we heard Billie's new owners had returned her.

They didn't say exactly what the problem was, but the word "stupid" was used. We now knew she was the perfect match for Ted. We collected her that day.

To say Ted and Billie hit it off from the start would be an understatement. After the initial bonding session in separate cages, the neutered Ted pounced on the neutered Billie and attempted his own bonding session. The fact he was sideways-on and Billie seemed more interested in her carrot spoke volumes.

After three more bonding attempts from various angles Ted gave up and concentrated on his own carrot.

Anyway, they're now happily settled in their hutch. Billie watched many times in wonder as Ted demonstrated how to get

Amorous Ted pounced on her to attempt a bonding session

from the top of the hutch to the bottom without using the ladder, generally landing on his head and rolling into a wall. Finally she strolled gracefully down the ladder, first time, with no instruction. Ted stared. His new bride had taught him a valuable life lesson. I'm not sure how much longer he could have survived that ladder without Billie.

So we were unable to help with the bunny crisis, but at least we saved one rabbit this week, even if was our own…

TED MISSES THE POINT

Ted's up to his old tricks again – this time Cleo the hamster is in the firing line

My rabbit Ted has appeared in my column before and I may have given the impression that Ted isn't exactly the sharpest knife in the drawer. In fact, I labelled him The World's Dumbest Rabbit.

Well, the lop-eared Ted is now settled in with his bride Billie, and the pair of them rub along nicely – though I have, on occasion, observed Billie eyeing Ted with great suspicion. I think it's suspicion anyway; being a rabbit she doesn't have a massive range of facial expressions, but those wide-eyed long stares in Ted's direction suggest suspicion, bewilderment and, I can't help but notice, a level of disdain.

It's not really surprising. Billie is slim and elegant, with an unmistakably female face – a bit like one of those cartoon rabbit girls who often cause Bugs Bunny's eyes to pop out of his head and his heart to visibly hammer against his chest.

Ted, on the other hand, has the scruffy demeanor of a man who's just got out of bed and can't remember where he is or if he owns a hair brush. He also has a habit of suddenly keeling over sideways, instantly asleep as his head hits the hay. It's this odd tendency to suddenly fall asleep in the middle of whatever he's doing that seems to alarm Billie the most.

Well, actually, no, an incident that happened earlier this week alarmed her the most – and we were quite surprised too.

It was indoor playtime in our lounge for our two nose-twitching friends, and for our hamster Cleo, who rolled merrily around them in her hamster-ball. Now, after Ted's yearning for a female rabbit companion, and our great relief at finding one who'd actually accept him, you'd expect him to show her a little attention and affection, wouldn't you? Her, not a hamster-ball.

Ted mounted that hamster ball with a level of energy and enthusiasm we had no idea he even possessed, much to the horror of the hamster inside. A clearly stunned Cleo quickened her pace, removing her rapidly rolling ball from beneath the enamored Ted, leaving him, for the briefest of moments, standing on his hind legs

Billie's stares suggest a level of bewilderment, suspicion and disdain

and performing unsavoury Twerking dance moves.

Then, inevitably with a sudden lack of hamster-ball to support him, he pitched forwards and fell flat on his face. Billie munched on some hay as she watched. Ted wasn't bothered though. He was already asleep.

Rabbits can be "more intelligent than dogs" the girl at the pet shop claimed when persuaded us to take Ted off her hands. Really? He mounts a hamster ball when he has a female rabbit right next to him, still can't always work out how to get from the top of the hutch to the bottom without hitting the floor at breakneck speed, and sleeps upside down with his head in his food bowl. More intelligent than a dog? He's not even more intelligent than me…

TAKING ON THE WORLD

Who needs TV when you have the world's dumbest pet to entertain you?

I decided it would be interesting to go on a two hour Tedwatch. Ted is my pet rabbit, and a genuine contender for the world's dumbest pet. I see Ted engaged in so many inexplicably stupid activities during the course of any given week that I decided, in the name of column research, to observe Ted closely for an afternoon. This had nothing to do with it being a lovely sunny day, and definitely not because of Lorraine's suggestion I help with her telemarketing project. Lorraine's accusations to the contrary are absolutely scandalous.

During my two-hour fruit-juice and sunbathing session… er, my two-hour academic leporine-observation tenure, I have to report I've never seen a creature involved in so many head-on collisions with inanimate objects in my life.

From the moment I opened the hutch door to allow Ted and his long-suffering wife Billie out into their sun-soaked run, it was clear that Ted was absolutely determined that any obstacle that stood in his way should remain in his way. While Billie neatly sidestepped through the half-open door, Ted hurtled down his carpeted ramp and ran straight into the door-jamb with the ferocity of a charging rhinoceros. Three times. I'm sure it was only a lucky deflection on the third hit sending him sprawling onto the grass that prevented him headbutting his hutch door all afternoon.

19

Once out, he tumbled into his food bowl. He seemed to quite like it and settled down for a nap, his head nestled in a pile of nuggets. Billie looked on, her nose twitching in a kind of seriously unimpressed but still curious manner.

I dutifully made my notes. Tedwatch: three head-on collisions, now asleep in foodbowl. Moving into third minute. I decided I'd best nip inside for more paper – two A4 sheets clearly weren't going to be enough.

Five minutes later he woke, ate some of the nuggets he'd been dozing in, and with a kick of his giant back feet ran straight into Billie broadside, catapulting her over his back. Now she was impressed.

The next ten minutes were mercifully uneventful. Billie settled down for a long Ted-grooming session, something that seemed to relax him and, apart from Billie receiving the occasional kick in the face when Ted forgot he was being groomed and went for a quick

A lucky deflection on the third hit sent him sprawling outside

neck-scratch, went very well.

Then things began to liven up. Ted, clearly also forgetting that he'd been neutered, decided he'd "go for it". There ensued a three-minute Benny Hill-style chase around the run, during which Ted managed to miss Billie with every jump for her back, finally crashing into his bowl again.

The afternoon ended with Ted attempting to eat his own carpet, Billie looking on in much the same way Lorraine would if I started eating our lounge carpet (Lorraine has smaller ears, and I prefer lino).

So, an enjoyable if mildly alarming afternoon on Tedwatch. It's something I'll definitely be repeating. The very next time we take on a few hours' telemarketing work.

END OF THE BUNNYMOON

Ted's appetite gets the better of him and his new bride decides to take action

There's been a bit of friction between our love-bunnies, Ted and Billie. I suppose when two previously single members of any species, rabbit, human or otherwise, accustomed to their own space, move in together, there has to be a period of getting used to each other's ways. Inevitably at some point, something one does will upset the other.

In the case of the rabbits outside our window, this something was that Ted ate Billie's bed. Guaranteed to cause friction, that. If somebody ate my bed, I'm pretty sure I'd struggle not to at least bring the subject up.

Billie liked to sleep in a petshop-bought multi-coloured cardboard tunnel. Ted would sleep alongside it and the two were co-existing very nicely. Then Ted discovered that his partner's bed was just-about edible. Within a few days, Billie's bed had vanished.

There followed a short period of sulking. Of course Ted was blissfully oblivious to Billie's displeasure, having a level of awareness only slightly higher than a slab of concrete. But when Billie stopped grooming him, it finally dawned.

Billie and Ted previously had a give-and-take arrangement – Billie would give Ted lots of licks, nibbles and rubs… and Ted would take them. Billie put up with it. Not now he'd eaten the bed, though.

They'd had much the same relationship with food. If there were two pieces of broccoli, Ted would eat one, then he'd eat the second straight from Billie's mouth. This wasn't your romantic Lady and the Tramp-style spaghetti sharing – he'd just start munching away and finally rip the last piece of broccoli from between her teeth and leg it. Again though, this all stopped. Billie fought him off and Ted watched her eat in wonder.

Ted was most concerned about the lack of grooming. He began constantly shoving his head beneath Billie's mouth, hoping she'd give in and nibble his ears. Finally, he got more than he bargained for – Billie brought both front claws forward and went for the top of Ted's head like she was trying to dig a hole. A shocked Ted ran into a corner. A few moments later, Billie began playing with a plastic food bowl, lifting it in her teeth and then flipping it with her paws. Ted watched, fascinated.

Finally he hopped back towards her, wanting to join in the fun.

Billie watched him coming, picked the bowl up in her teeth, tried a couple of practice swings, and then proceeded to smack Ted straight over the head with it. This was no accident, as proved by constant repetition. She must have hit him eight times before Ted realised he was under attack and retreated.

The war is now over and, miraculously, Billie appears to have knocked some sense into him. He no longer steals her food and grooming has become far more mutual. We've also bought Billie a new bed… which I now notice has a sizeable bite mark in the corner. She can't have hit him hard enough. 🐾

After a couple of practice swings she smacked him over the head

A FESTIVE CASCADE

Chris is spreading festive joy and a goodwill to all his furry friends

It's Christmas time and I'm on my festive pet-sitting rounds, bringing turkey slices and catnip stockings to all my feline friends.

Some of my favourite visits haven't been just to a cat though, but to the Feckless Five, mentioned a couple of weeks ago – two rabbits who are lupine doppelgangers for my own semi-sentient disaster of a rabbit, Ted; two guinea pigs who live in the same large enclosure and run rings round the rabbits (literally) and the token cat, sky-diving ginger maniac Fred Flintstone.

Of course, the tenants of the pen wouldn't really be interested in turkey and catnip, so I had some veg and herb treats for them.

Knowing the pen situation as I do, I realised that simply throwing the treats in like a herbaceous hand-grenade would result in the guinea pigs eating the whole lot while the two Teds sat trying to figure out what was happening. I needed to get into the pen and hand-feed the Teds before all the food had been g-pigged.

It didn't really go very well. Firstly, I failed to judge the height of the pen's step when manoeuvring through its low wire and wood doorframe. I thus entered in something approaching a forward roll, landing knee first in a large water-bowl and transferring most of its contents to the front of my trousers.

I also succeeded in dropping my armful of herbs and vegetables all over the pen floor. The guinea pigs gleefully snatched at every falling treat.

This scatter-gun approach to feeding time was the exact opposite of my original plan, and I began scrambling to my feet to rescue food for the Teds. It was at this point that the Teds noticed me.

I'd fallen loudly into their home, shouting and cursing as I landed in their water bowl, and there hadn't been so much as a flicker, but now suddenly they were fully awake.

In the next few slightly surreal moments, I looked on as they suddenly launched into action, bowling their miniature cousins aside and whipping away a share of the food.

As I watched in wonder, a famous Christmas Carol crept unbidden into my mind, albeit with slightly changed words: Fear not said me for mighty Teds had seized their kale and thyme.

Suddenly I felt about as Christmassy as a partially drenched fat

I entered the pen in something approaching a forward roll

bloke standing in a rabbit pen could possibly be.

Was that snowflakes falling into the branches of the garden's tall pine trees? Well, actually no, a single ginger cat began falling through the branches of the garden's conifer trees, but that would have to do.

The Christmas picture was complete. A feeling of goodwill to all – cats, rabbits and guinea pigs alike, settled upon me. That was until I realised one of the guinea pigs was eating my shoe lace. A feeling of goodwill to all – cats and rabbits alike, settled upon me.

Have a great Christmas, and if you're a pet owner, remember to give all your wonderful furry friends a special treat of their own on the big day. Merry Christmas. 🐾

THE WIND IN THE BUSHES

Ted the rabbit has an excellent defence mechanism against potential predators!

B illie, wife of Ted the unofficial "world's dumbest rabbit", is a bunny who doesn't like to be out after dark. The moment night begins to fall, Billie is watching our every move from her hutch. Wherever you are in the house, Billie will be watching you. She seems to know which window you'll appear at next, because she's already staring at it when you get there – hoping we'll be out to fetch her soon, transferring her and her oblivious mate into their nice warm indoor double-cage for the night.

The fact Billie is so desperate to come indoors every night makes it all the more baffling that she attempted her own version of the *Great Escape* the other day.

To be fair Ted's been going through one of his "unwholesome" stages of late, and this time he's opted for over-enthusiastic flatulence. Being trapped in a confined space with him would probably make any rabbit on earth decide to take their chances with the foxes.

What was unbelievable, though, was that while she attempted an escape, the slow thinking, slow- reacting and almost non-moving Ted actually achieved one.

It all began at dusk, and Billie was performing her usual array of rabbit contradictions – watching us intently for half an hour and clawing frantically at the hutch door every time she caught our eye,

but refusing to hop into her rabbit carrier for her inbound trip.

No matter what incentives were offered, carrots, broccoli and the like, Billie remained stubbornly rooted to the rear wall of the hutch.

Finally, after closing off every other available direction, I moved the open carrier slowly towards Billie.

For a moment she seemed to go into submission and started hopping towards me but then suddenly, with a blistering turn of pace, she was round the carrier, through my legs and heading for the dense garden bushes – if she managed to get in there we'd never find her.

I had no choice but to perform a full length dive across the garden… well, I say dive, most would call it a bellyflop face-first into an inch of mud, but at least it had the desired effect. As I lay with my hands securely around Billie's midriff, I was horrified to see Ted casually ambling past me. I bolted Billie into her carrier and legged it after Ted.

I was quite horrified to see Ted casually ambling past me

I looked at the sizeable mass of bushes in despair. This was serious. Any domestic rabbit out on its own is immediately in severe predator-danger, never mind a rabbit who'd happily walk up to a lion and sniff its feet. And then I heard it. FLARP! And then again! Vile cabbage-smelling flatulence had suddenly become a good thing. FLARP… got him.

Three minutes later he was indoors with Billie, although I'm not sure she appreciated the fact.

As I fed them both treats and loaded up on bedding-hay for the night, my eyes watering slightly at a final and definitive blast from Ted, I began to wonder why I'd been so worried about him being out for the night. I'm fairly sure the foxes would've given him a very wide berth. 🐾

GAME OF THRONES

Who will emerge victorious from the inter-species battle for the best seat?

I'm currently embroiled in a three-way power struggle involving me, an alpha male and a zeta male who doesn't know he is a zeta male, or even male… in fact, I don't think he really knows what he is.

Yes, while others take part in high-powered business, ruthless social climbing and political power broking, I'm jockeying for position with a cat and a semi-sentient rabbit.

Bodmin is the huge black stray cat who decided he lived in our back bedroom and, after observing his massive claws and sabre-tooth razor fangs, we decided not to bring the matter up with him. In fact, we fed him three times a day, provided him with a radiator bed, warm cushions and a loving home. And, being a cat, he obviously wanted revenge for this.

This vengeful petulance first manifested itself at the food bowl. Suddenly Felix and Whiskas weren't good enough – Bodmin wanted cooked chicken and tuna. If he didn't get it, he'd deliberately upend his bowl. After a few such incidents, he began looking at Ted the rabbit with a worrying eagerness.

The real trouble started when Bodmin began spending more time in the living room. He quickly decided that my place on the sofa should be his – every time I stood up, he'd be straight into my place. I'd attempt to remove him; he'd attempt to remove my hand.

The other problem is that the lounge is where Ted and Billie come to run free for an hour or so every evening. Well, Billie runs free while Ted just sits staring at his favourite part of the wall.

With Bodmin's intentions towards Ted seemingly a bit dicey, it became necessary to watch him like a hawk.

Lorraine's good at watching things like a hawk. I'm not. Within

seconds of Lorraine leaving the room one evening, I vaguely noticed out of the corner of my eye that Bodmin seemed to have Ted trapped in a headlock. Jumping up to save a rabbit who had no clue he needed saving was a mistake. Bodmin had tricked me, shooting across the room and onto my sofa-spot before I could travel two steps.

Battle had commenced, with Bodmin and I taking our latest fight down onto the carpet, when a suddenly enlivened Ted sauntered across the room, hopped onto a footstool and thence to the contested sofa-spot.

I looked at Bodmin, Bodmin looked at me. For the briefest moment, we were united… but then he nipped my ear.

He found his ability to jump was hampered by a 4lb rabbit

As fighting resumed, Ted suddenly appeared on Bodmin's back. The cat looked horrified. As he tried to reach the safety of a high place, he found his ability to jump severely hampered by a dopey 4lb rabbit clinging to his back.

Bodmin broke free and made it to the top of the wall unit. As Billie and I looked on incredulously, Ted hopped back onto the sofa and settled down to wash. The rabbit had won. I'd been defeated by a cat who'd himself been defeated by a zeta rabbit.

I need to think of a new category for myself. Somewhere south of zeta. 🐾

LOVE STRUCK BUNNIES

It takes time to make a marriage work – as rabbits Ted and Billie are finding out

Every single time he wakes up, usually a couple of hours after keeling over sideways into his food bowl, Ted will sit up bleary-eyed, notice his live-in-partner-rabbit Billie somewhere in the hutch and go into shock. Every single time.

The fact that Billie has now lived with him for over 18 months doesn't seem to make the slightest bit of difference. He's still amazed to see her.

For a rabbit who sees making any type of movement at all as a difficult life-choice, his sudden animation is quite alarming. He'll sit bolt upright and stare unblinkingly at Billie, his normal squint rapidly becoming a wide-eyed stare as his ears prick up and his nose goes into twitching overdrive. He'll then carefully approach Billie down the length of the hutch, stopping stock-still whenever Billie glances up from her hay munching and casually noting his advance.

Then, upon finally reaching her, he'll generally do something totally pointless, like attempting to mount her.

This very much annoys Billie. Not many people like being mounted by a semi-sentient flatulent rabbit halfway through their lunch, and Billie's no different. Her next move will be to deftly spring forwards and back-kick Ted in the face.

As he reels uncertainly on his giant back feet, she'll often grab a

food bowl between her teeth and smack him round the head with it. As a romantic gesture it's probably slightly misguided but as an ardour-dampener it's spot-on. I'm not sure if it's impact-related but at this point Ted often seems to shake himself back to reality and finally calm down.

He'd save himself so much hardship if only he could remember exactly what Billie is capable of.

All this makes me wonder if Ted has any idea whatsoever who exactly Billie is, where she came from and when she turned up in his home. I still remember the day we brought Billie home. We set off to Slough with a feeling of happy excitement, and it'll be a long time before you hear anybody say that again. After completing adoption paperwork and only narrowly passing the "fit and proper owner" test we collected a young and beautiful Billie and took her home to begin a new life with the scruffy urchin that is Ted, like a lamb to the slaughter.

As a romantic gesture it is probably slightly misguided

Ted of course, won't remember that happy day or, apparently, any of the 543 days since, but I'm sure Billie does. How she now feels about it is another matter, but I'm sure she remembers it.

Anyway, I've probably painted a full enough picture of Ted and Billie's harmonious marriage since that fateful day, but in all truth they wouldn't be without one another, and when you see them cuddle up together you realise that.

He might be a scruffy, slightly smelly, lump of a spouse, but Billie loves him.

I think my other half Lorraine feels much the same about me.

Chris Pascoe's Fun Tales

FANCY THAT!

Rabbit facts to make you go "wow"

Rabbits' ears can pick up sounds from every direction and are capable of hearing from two directions at the same time.

The Wallace & Gromit film _Curse of the Were-Rabbit_ used 2.8 tons of Plasticine and they got through 1000 baby wipes per week to wipe it off the animators' fingers.

Angora rabbits are sheared several times a year.

Bambi and Thumper were voiced by children, a break with the normal practice of using adults mimicking youngsters.

A rabbit takes approximately 18 naps per day.

In Tim Burton's version of *Alice In Wonderland* released in 2010, the White Rabbit is given the name Nivens McTwisp and is voiced by Michael Sheen.

The Tales Of Peter Rabbit was the first of Beatrix Potter's books to be published, in 1902.

Rabbits can have 800 children, grandchildren and great-grandchildren during their lifetimes.

Rabbits can jump over 2 feet vertically, and up to 9 feet horizontally.

Bugs Bunny was the first cartoon character to ever appear on a US stamp.

Richard Adams, who wrote *Watership Down*, based Hazel and the band of rabbits he leads on members of his army unit during World War II.

SOAP ON A DOPEY BUNNY

A smelly rabbit, a confused vet and a hysterical wife... how will Chris cope?

Ted's first ever bath became an urgent necessity when my wife Lorraine opened his hutch only to be hit full blast in the face by a smell grenade.

I won't go into detail here, but let's just say Ted's rear end was in a bit of a state. After looking up the problem (no no, not like that... on the internet) I took website advice, ran a very shallow bath and booked a vet's appointment. I always do what websites tell me to do, and anyway Ted was due his annual vaccinations.

The bath went OK, apart from Ted trying to drink it, and we soon found ourselves at the local vets.

After a brief examination, the vet disappeared to show Ted to her colleagues – she probably wanted to check what on earth she was looking at.

She returned a few minutes later, without Ted, glanced down at her notes and then looked up at me.

"So, eh, Dave, is it?"

"No, it's Chris," I said, smiling.

"Ah OK, sorry."

Lorraine walked into the room at this moment, having been chatting in the waiting room. The vet sat us both down to explain the situation.

"OK," she said solemnly. "We can't vaccinate Chris today

because he's had medication for his messy bottom."

Lorraine looked bemused for just one moment, and then her face began to crumple into a desperately suppressed grin. My attempts at a quick name correction were drowned out by Lorraine's muffled laughter and the vet continuing,

"Chris is also pretty fat, which may be why he isn't washing properly. So, a diet – and also keep him indoors for a few days so he doesn't attract flies."

Lorraine's face contorted and she ran from the room laughing.

"Um, just so you know, I'm Chris; the rabbit's called Ted."

The vet regarded me carefully before simply nodding and continuing her instructions. Bearing in mind this was the same vet I'd lied to about working as a security guard and owning a "company dog", they were probably expecting something like this.

Incidentally, this type of reaction is typical of Lorraine – at the optician's recently the assistant kept readjusting my glasses over

"Keep him indoors for a few days so he doesn't attract flies"

and over, saying that the problem was that I had an abnormally wide head and my eyes were too close together. I'm not sure exactly what type of person this made me sound like, but Lorraine eventually had to leave the premises. We could both hear her screams of laughter outside the door.

Anyway, Ted returned a few minutes later – they'd given him a bath. That poor, poor rabbit, I thought.

Not sure why I worried, though, he's back in his hutch munching hay and seemingly oblivious to the fact he's had his first two baths in one day.

His partner Billie seems well aware, though – it's her look of total relief that gives it away.

HOLLYWOOD BUNBUSTER

Could the bunnies really be movie star dopplegangers? It's a "really cool" idea

A pparently there are two major Hollywood movies, about our rabbits. It was only when my daughter Maya introduced Ted and Billie to a visiting friend that we were made aware of this.

"Ha ha," laughed her friend on meeting our favourite lop-eared lothario and his long suffering mate, "Great names!"

This surprised us all. We'd never really considered the names Ted and Billie to be clever or funny. In fact, Billie already had her name when she moved in and we thought it would be rude to change it.

"They're not the Bill and Ted are they!?" she continued, chortling away.

We'd always assumed them to be the Billie and Ted, but now we had doubts.

"Great movies! You're so cool naming them that," she concluded, fist-bumping the side of my head.

I'd just been called cool by a teenager – this was completely unexpected. I had to find out what I'd done that was cool, before the opposite became apparent. Also, that fist-bump to the temple had been a bit hard I thought – I needed to sit down for a minute or two.

So, killing two birds with one stone, I slumped in front of

Billie & Ted's Excellent Adventures!

the computer and googled 'Bill and Ted', exactly the way she'd repeated their names.

I was quite taken aback to see thousands of entries relating to the popular Hollywood blockbusters *Bill & Ted's Excellent Adventure* and *Bill & Ted's Bogus Journey*.

Ha, I thought, as if Ted could ever be likened to any Hollywood star. Here was a lad who spent the first four months of his life unaware his hutch had an upstairs.

I read the first line of the synopsis 'In the small town of San Dimas, a few miles away from Los Angeles, there are two nearly brain dead teenage boys going by the names of Bill and Ted.'

Nearly brain dead?

OK, I conceded, there's a definite connection here.

With a slightly spinning head and the miracle of technology at my fingertips, I proceeded to watch the whole of the first movie there and then. I sat in awe as I realised just how much screen Ted

Nearly brain dead? Ok, there's a definite connection here

was like rabbit Ted – he even had a lop-eared style haircut. I also hadn't realised just how much rabbit Ted could be likened to a blissfully unaware spaced out dope-head (at this moment I caught a glimpse of Ted through my window, munching a carrot then keeling over sideways into a pile of dandelion stalks, immediately asleep – instant affirmation).

Although there was very little in it, I felt that screen Bill was the slightly more capable and lively of the two, so this comparison also works. Only loosely though because rabbit Billie is 100% the more capable and lively of our two, but fulfils the role of sidekick, even if her 'side-kicks' are more commonly back-kicks to Ted's head.

As the movie drew to a close, the comparisons had to stop – screen Bill & Ted ended up saving the world.

I can't see my Ted doing that anytime soon.

COMPLETELY POTTY!

Chris contemplates whether Ted the rabbit has an easier life he does...

While I'm slaving long hours, sitting on sofas, stroking cats and watching TV, I often dream of one day winning the lottery and being able to leave all this hardship behind.

Actually, not exactly behind me. I'll still do exactly the same things but with two major differences. 1. No-one will be paying me to do it, and 2. I'll live somewhere with enough room for a great big shed in which to do the lounging and TV-watching… the man-dream.

I'll also have one of those microchip catflaps in the shed door so only my cats could join me, and not that maniac ginger Tom from down the road who sprays my clothes while I sleep.

For now, I can only hope for sheds and urine-free clothing, but my rabbit Ted is already living the man dream. By simple virtue of residing in a hutch, Ted is spending most of his life pottering around in a virtual shed.

Ted fully immerses himself in this wonderful lifestyle – he often fully immerses himself in his water bowl too, but that's not intentional – eating, snoozing, sleeping and watching the world go by. Or his case, watching the cats go by, which is much better than them dropping in. Not that he'd realise that – but even I was surprised the other day to glance out of the kitchen window and spot the lop-eared lounger taking it all to a whole new level.

Ted was sitting on the toilet reading the newspaper. Well, I say reading it, but let's remember this is a rabbit we're talking about here, and not a bright one at that. Ted was sitting on the toilet eating the newspaper. A slight usage error on his part, I know, but he'd still achieved the benchmark – sitting in the shed, on the toilet, with the newspaper. Valhalla!

The toilet in question, by the way, is an elaborate corner unit litter tray that Lorraine thought would enhance the rabbits' quality of life, and it may well have done so during its first three months in the hutch, if only Ted had in any way understood what it was for.

He'd sit munching hay, staring in total bewilderment as his partner-rabbit, the pristine Billie, would hop into the tray, carry out her ablutions, flush, and hop away. (OK, I admit there's no flush.) You could almost see Ted's mind whirring as he continued to stare at the tray long after Billie had vacated it. Then, just when you

We're talking about a rabbit and not a very bright one at that

think he might possibly have cracked it, he'll soil himself while still sitting three feet from the toilet. Brilliant!

Not today. Today Ted was using that toilet… in the Ted-Shed, and all was right with the world.

Actually though, not wanting to burst bubbles here but the image of Ted living the man-dream has a major flaw. The whole man-shed thing is based on the idea of personal space, a retreat from everything and everyone. So, yes, Ted has a shed, but his wife lives in it with him.

That's Hades, not Valhalla.

LADY AND THE CHUMP

Who would have thought that a treat could be so tricky?

The most romantic moment in movie history is of course the spaghetti-eating scene in *Lady and the Tramp*. The film's would-be sweetheart canines unwittingly begin eating either end of one long strand of spaghetti, only for their faces to be drawn together, until the scene ends with a blushing Lady coyly fluttering her eyelids.

My rabbit Ted attempted to re-enact this scene the other day. Two three-inch- long rabbit treatsticks had been pushed into the hutch, one for Ted and one for his live-in partner, girl-rabbit Billie. Completely failing to notice his own treatstick, Ted rushed forward, trampling it into the hay, to take a closer look at Billie's.

A couple of nose twitches later, Ted realised he may be missing out on something, and that something was disappearing into Billie's mouth.

With uncharacteristic speed, he suddenly dived face first at Billie's teeth, desperately attempting to retrieve the half inch of treat still protruding. What followed was a very odd scene indeed.

Billie stood firm, gripping the treat like her life depended on it, but Ted had the other end; it was stalemate. The two rabbits stood nose to nose, glaring into one another's eyes. If Ted had intended this to be romantic, things were going very wrong indeed. Billie suddenly tugged at the treat, jolting Ted's head violently forward.

47

He tugged back, infuriating Billie. The to-ing and fro-ing continued for at least ten seconds, looking very much like a bizarre dance routine.

I decided at this point it was time to intervene before things got nasty for Ted. I opened the hutch door and began gently passing a new treatstick under Billie's nose. Billie's eyes followed it back and forth. Just when I thought she might opt for a change of treat, Ted dived full length at the new treat, completely missing it and clamping his teeth down on my finger! Billie, stunned, first stared at me in confusion, then noticed Ted had something new in his mouth and, entering into the spirit of the thing, dived in too.

My finger was now clamped between two rabbit's teeth and they started pulling.

Lorraine walked in, took one look at the situation and calmly asked, "What are you doing to those rabbits?"

Five minutes later, sticking plaster on finger, I pondered how

The two rabbits stood nose to nose, glaring at each other

simply giving two rabbits a treat could have ended in such carnage.

As a footnote to all this – as a writer, I do the normal writer thing and make notes about absolutely everything. My method is to email myself from my mobile phone, so that the note goes straight back to my computer.

If you're thinking to yourself, He's a bit more high-tech than I thought, think again. I didn't check the recipient address carefully enough. Consequently a fairly new customer named Christopher Parker received a quite alarming email, containing nothing but the words Two rabbits kiss-dancing with 3 inch treat-stick.

I've since emailed an apology, but I think I might be on his blocked-sender list.

TOTAL HEAD BANGER!

Even reaching into the fridge, Chris isn't safe from his randomly destructive rabbit

My rabbit almost knocked me out with a beer can…"
That's not a standard conversation opener, is it?
Yet this was exactly what I found myself saying to the postman this morning. As I'm sure you'll already have guessed, the rabbit involved wasn't Billie, our demure, normal Dutch, but rather our barely sentient lop-eared lunatic Ted.

But how could a rabbit knock you out with a flying beer can – even a rabbit like Ted? In an extension of his reading-on-the-loo shed-man persona (I know that will seem a fairly odd sentence to anyone who didn't read that particular column), did he down a beer with a giant belch, scrunch it up and throw at my head from his shed window?

No, obviously not. Don't be so silly. It was a full can, for a start, and I'd just seconds earlier removed it from the fridge.

The problem here is that our fridge sits under a utility-room work surface ledge, and on top of this ledge sit Ted and Billie's bad-weather sleeping quarters, a single storey cage eight feet long.

Deciding I'd like some cheese with my beer, I popped the can on top of Ted's cage and bent to grab the cheese from the fridge.

Ted, waking slowly from yet another impromptu nap, noticed me place something on his roof, and for reasons known only to him, jumped at it. I heard rather than saw him hurl himself at the

51

top of his cage, and the next thing I knew, I was hit squarely on the back of the head by a falling can of beer.

In a split second, I went from a kneeling position to face down spread-eagled on the utility room floor. It hit me so hard I found myself blinking as I lay there, trying to work out what had hit me.

Typically, my daughter Maya chose this moment to walk in. She stopped in her tracks and regarded the scene.

"Mummy!" she shouted, "Daddy's drunk again!"

Again? One incident four years ago, after a party, when I tried to park her Barbie convertible sports-car in next door's drive and couldn't stop giggling, and now… "he's drunk again." Great.

After telling my tale of woe to the postman, who smiled and shook his head in bemusement, I found myself wondering if there were any statistics on how many people suffer rabbit-related injuries each year? An internet safari was in order.

I was hit squarely on the back of the head by a falling can of beer

My search on rabbit-related injuries came up with an array of disturbing results involving a very different type of rabbit so I quickly tried a different phrase, How many people are killed or injured due to rabbit attacks?

Not surprisingly, I couldn't find a single result. Just me, then. However, the following intriguing suggestion did pop up on my screen: Did Rabbits Kill the Neanderthals?

This was a wholly unexpected sentence, even more unlikely than my opening line here and definitely needs looking into. Ted vs The Neanderthals. Now there's a match-up. 🐾

TORVILL AND TED!

Unleash the rabbits – but preferably not on a slippery kitchen floor

During the winter, our garden becomes more marsh than lawn. The sun doesn't quite make it over next door's rooftop, so everything soon becomes a just a little on the muddy side.

I'd ask our neighbour to demolish the top storey of his house but, considering our heavyweight cat Bodmin started work on that front a few months ago, accidentally removing three tiles as he pranced across the rooftops like a performing hippo, I don't think the suggestion would go down well.

The missing lawn is a big problem for Ted (world's dumbest rabbit, self-crowned Prince of Idiots and general floppy-eared menace) and his demure partner-rabbit Billie. They live in an indoor hutch at this time of year, but need to go outside for exercise. This doesn't work well when the garden's a mudbath – Billie just stares at it in horror and refuses to move, while Ted hops happily off into the abyss, looking more like the Lindt Chocolate Bunny with every leap.

So it was decided the rabbits would have to roam the house. With us. The only sizeable room is our kitchen, so it was quickly danger-proofed and then, with much trepidation… we unleashed the rabbits.

As the delighted pair went bounding across the floor, we became

aware of an unforeseen problem. Their claws, in need of a trim, were incapable of attaining any sort of grip on the smooth lino. While Billie instantly grasped the problem and stopped, Ted hurtled onwards, eventually skidding three feet sideways into our vegetable rack, bringing down a sudden shower of carrots and lettuce.

As Ted sat dazed, half a carrot perched jauntily between his ears, Billie's nose twitched in surprise – was it really raining carrots?

I don't know – maybe it was the moment, maybe it was the moonlight, or maybe it was the lettuce, but Billie forgot all about maintaining her balance and ran straight at Ted's salad-landslide.

Unable to stop, she clattered into Ted at speed, ending up sprawled over his back and began munching on his carrot headwear.

Billie's nose twitched in surprise – was it really raining carrots?

Ted was having none of it. For two years, he'd been the one continually trying to get on top (and failing). Now not only was Billie lying on him, she was also eating his carrot.

What followed was an incredible scene. It started with a fight as Ted struggled and kicked his way from under Billie, mutated into a peculiar dance as both leaped around not really knowing what they were doing, and became a free-for-all as they clambered for vegetables while constantly sliding into one another. It was *Strictly Come Dine With Me Dancing on Ice… with rabbits*. Featuring Torvill & Ted.

The melée ended as it began, Ted flat on his face and Billie happily munching a carrot. Ted was facing away from the vegetables – he seemed to have forgotten they were there.

THE TROUBLE WITH DOORS...

When one door closes, another opens – but Ted can't deal with that either…

My lop-eared disaster bunny Ted has been having issues with doors. While most of us sail through life, walking through doors without problems, Ted sees them as immovable objects.

Ted's live-in partner rabbit Billie has been the main cause of Ted's latest woes. She's developed a habit of hopping into their run, turning, and throwing all her weight against the hutch door, thus slamming it in Ted's face as he attempts to follow her.

All Ted need do at this point of course, is simply push the door open and walk through it, but this doesn't seem to have occurred to him. Instead he regards the closed door in wonder for a few moments, then falls over sideways into a deep sleep, which is Ted's default action when faced with any form of problem-solving.

Because of this new development, we decided to cut a hole in the hutch's wooden front wall.

Billie immediately spotted the potential of this unexpected new doorway, and hopped through it with wild abandon. Ted spent three days doing nothing but stare at it. The real problems began on day four when he finally attempted to use it.

Things started OK, with Ted jumping into the hole and slamming his front paws down on the grass outside. It soon became clear though, that he had no idea what to do next. There he remained –

front paws outside, rear legs inside, belly grounded on the lip of the hole. Subsequent attempts saw a slight improvement, in that upon reaching the halfway point, he began clawing at the grass in an attempt to drag himself forward.

Unfortunately Ted couldn't get any real purchase on the grass so the whole thing just became a static ploughing exercise. Pondering the problem, I popped a doormat outside the hole to give him something to grab hold of.

This almost worked – Ted grabbed it, pulled it upwards, then repeatedly smacked himself in the face with it.

OK, I thought, a heavier-duty mat is required here, and duly provided one. Success! Well, partial success. Ted's current technique involves grabbing the mat, snagging his front claws in it, pulling with all his might, and then performing a perfect forward roll into the run as his head and body leave his snagged paws behind. Brilliant.

The whole thing became a static ploughing exercise

Just to cap it all, I walked into the garden yesterday and found Ted standing upright at his wire hutch door. He also appeared to be waving at me.

I quickly surmised something was wrong. Seconds later I extracted Ted's raised and trapped paw from the mesh and pondered how much Ted must wish for a life without doors.

Being the world's dumbest rabbit, of course, means he wouldn't have considered that foxes would also quite like him to do away with his front door, but we can all dream, Ted lad, we can all dream… 🐾

A TRULY GIFTED TED

So just what do you get for the rabbit who has everything…?

So, with Christmas just round the corner, every gift is wrapped, the house is draped from roof to foundations in festive lights, inflatable snow people inhabit every inch of lawn, and all the cards are in the Royal Mail's capable hands.

Actually, none of that's true. I've done absolutely nothing. I haven't even wrapped the rabbits' presents yet. Yes, I give gifts to rabbits.

When we handed out the presents last year, our barely sentient bunny Ted (officially the world's dumbest rabbit) managed to briefly convince us he wasn't so dumb after all. Please note the word "briefly" in that sentence.

Ted led us to reach that totally misguided conclusion by doing something unexpected – he unwrapped his own present. When handed the carefully wrapped package, he reacted with crazed excitement, began ripping frantically at the Easter Bunny wrapping paper (well, you trying getting Christmas wrapping paper with rabbits on it) and didn't even fall asleep on the job once. He seemed to understand, really understand, that this was for him, it was a present, and it was exciting!

We couldn't believe it, thinking at last here was a sign of comprehension and intelligence. Our hopes dissipated as soon as his present was unveiled. Ted totally ignored the delicious treat

inside, and spent the next ten minutes eating the wrapping paper.

His live-in-partner-girl-rabbit Billie, meanwhile, was showing no interest in her own parcel, pointedly sitting with her back to it. It was only when Ted turned his attention to her present, that her attitude changed – and not in a nice way. Billie's nose began twitching, one ear pricked up (and that's a lot of ear to prick up) and then, without even looking over her shoulder, she suddenly back-kicked Ted down the length of the hutch.

A very Merry Christmas with baubles on it Ted, from Thumper. Actually, Bambi's Thumper doesn't quite do her justice. I sometimes think Billie would've been a natural choice for those Kung Fu Panda movies.

As Ted tried to recover his composure and head casually back down the hutch, he stepped into his water bowl and upended it down his front. Just a few moments before, he'd been looking like such a promising prospect; now he was soaking wet, covered in

You try getting Christmas wrapping paper with rabbits on

hay and sawdust, and he'd just eaten his own wrapping paper. Never mind.

With last year's shenanigans in mind, we are giving them a joint gift this year, and one that won't be wrapped, mainly because it would need about two hundred rolls of paper. We've got them a shed. Ted's shed has always been a pipedream, but now he really has one, with a built in hutch, a small toilet cubicle and elevated rabbit-runs.

So it should be a very Merry Christmas for Ted and Billie, starting a new life in a new home with all mod cons. As long as Ted doesn't eat it, of course…

RABBIT PUNCH!

Dopey bunny Ted takes a fair bit of punishment in his quest for treats…

Y ou know the old saying "no pleasure without pain"? Well, our local garden centre seems to have applied the principle in one Cellophane-wrapped package.

They've recently extended their pet department to include more and more rabbit-related goods – a move probably based entirely on my own spending patterns – and included in that expansion are some very inventive rabbit "treats."

Regular readers may remember that my rabbits Billie and Ted (demure yet slightly violent princess and the world's dumbest lapin respectively) last received treats in their Christmas stocking. It didn't end well, with Ted eventually being back-kicked two feet across the hutch. As I said, Billie can be a bit feisty at times.

Well, their latest treat offering came from the aforementioned garden centre, who incidentally, also have a rather interesting member of staff – an extremely beautiful young lady who greets customers by rubbing her face against their legs. She then jumps onto any nearby garden furniture and demands to have her head stroked.

This behaviour is perfectly acceptable here because the staff member in question is a small black cat named Willow.

Willow first wandered in years ago, and the kind-hearted staff immediately took her in. She's lived at the centre ever since, becoming a bit of a tourist attraction, with customers often popping in just to see her.

Of course, it'd be rude to leave without buying anything, so Willow has a positive effect on sales figures too. So much so that when one particular manager a few years ago suggested that Willow should (say this in whispered tones) maybe... leave, he received word from above that HE was very welcome to leave if he so wished, but Willow would be going nowhere!

Anyway, back to the rabbits. Their latest treat was actually a whole bundle of treats, all held together by string and then suspended from the top of their hutch.

The first problem was that it hung like a swinging punch bag. So with Billie munching it from one side, and Ted from the other, the result was a wildly swinging pendulum which they appeared to use to smack each other in the face.

Ted took a haymaker of a carrot treat to the left ear

It started out quite tamely, as boxing matches often do, with a few mild cuffs and hooks, before Ted took a haymaker of a carrot treat to the left ear and was suddenly almost out on his feet.

I think Billie saw this, because she moved straight in for the knock-out, jabbing forward for a piece of apple and swinging the whole contraption forward in a devastating rabbit punch to the jaw (what other type of punch would it be?)

It all finished with Billie munching idly on her apple, Ted lying flat out asleep at her feet, the vanquished challenger yet again.

To complete the picture, the top loop of the hanging treat had settled lightly onto Billie's head – Queen Billie had finally crowned herself. 🐾

LET SLEEPING RABBITS LIE

Ted the rabbit fails to fully appreciate his state-of-the-art new penthouse hutch…

It's been a big week for the rabbit population of our household – all two of them; the demure and sophisticated, but ever so slightly psychotically violent female Billie, and her barely sentient partner Ted, the world's dumbest rabbit.

On Saturday we updated their tired old indoor living quarters to a brand new shiny and trendy open-plan hutch. It was to be Bill and Ted's Great Big Open-Plan Living Adventure.

As well as being spacious, it contains all mod cons, with everything the modern bunny-about-town could ever need, including built in indestructible food bowls, hanging water bottles, a cave-like bedroom and a luxury toilet.

Ted, of course, failed to appreciate any of this and within 10 seconds of moving in, lurched over sideways and lay snoring with half his ear in the food bowl. Now I don't know how you feel about body parts in your dinner, but being someone who needs to stop eating if I find even a hair in my food, I'd probably be pretty upset to find an ear in it – especially with a sleeping rabbit attached.

Billie and I are often on the same wavelength (being on the same wavelength as a rabbit is one of the things that's made my life such a mess) and it would appear that she decided to take quick and decisive action on the matter because, by Tuesday, Ted had to be taken to the vet suffering with, as described by our long-suffering

Home is where the carrot is

vet, "a huge abscess behind the left ear, probably caused by a bite from another rabbit". So, either the aforementioned decisive action or she must have thought he was a carrot.

Ted needed immediate surgery. We were told this could be very stressful for a rabbit and he'd probably go off his food for a few days and need hand-feeding. When we returned to collect him he was idly munching hay and watching the world go by. The vet couldn't believe how totally laid-back he'd been, calling him a "very strong-minded rabbit indeed".

Strong-minded? I have a feeling all this owed less to bravery than to a complete failure to understand the situation, but I decided to give him the benefit of the doubt…and a carrot.

He lurched over, falling asleep with his ear in the food bowl

On returning to his brand new penthouse hutch, Ted obviously decided he needed a bit of bed-rest and made full use of its hidey-hole bedroom for the first time – though not by crawling into it, but rather lying draped over it like a floppy-eared rug. Only Ted could be given a man-cave and sit on top of it.

After a little while of his dozing, I happened to be passing the hutch and had the misfortune to witness Ted rolling over blissfully in his sleep… continuing to roll, and dropping over the edge of his cave like a stone, straight onto Billie as she sat grazing at the food bowl below, thus pushing her face down into a pile of pellets and copiously covering her in dust and food crumbs.

We're looking out for signs of a new abscess on Ted. Shouldn't be long now… 🐾

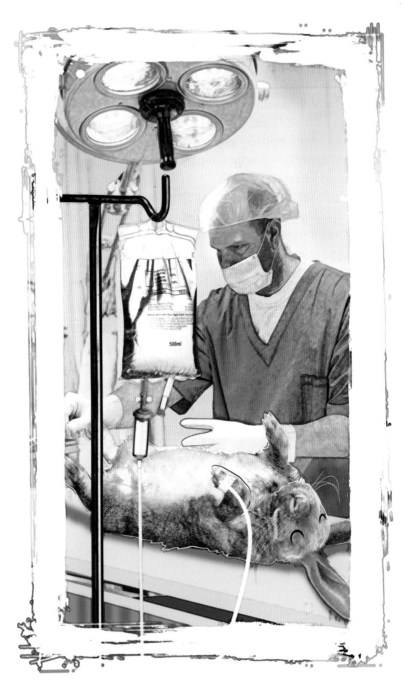

A NARROW ESCAPE

Chris and his hapless rabbit are well acquainted with vets...

I read a post on a social media site just recently which went something like this:

It is with great sadness that I must inform you that the "powers that be" have decided to revoke my medical licence, due to my becoming involved in a physical relationship with one of my patients. My years of medical training have been wasted. I now lose my lifelong vocation, and this village loses an excellent vet.

An unfortunate choice of words but this leads me neatly to my topic this week, vets. I spend a lot of time at veterinary clinics – not because doctors have refused to see me, but because of my catsitting work.

However, long before I became a catsitter, I was also spending an inordinate amount of time at the vets, courtesy of owning the accident-prone feline anti-hero of my books, Brum.

Our vet at the time developed a nervous tic at the very sight of Brum and I, reminiscent of the reaction of the Police Commissioner in *Pink Panther* movies when dealing with Inspector Clouseau.

Our most frequent vet-visitor nowadays is Ted, our generally semi-conscious rabbit.

Oh, if only vets gave air-miles, or even hair-miles. Regular readers may recall that Ted needed surgery a couple of weeks ago, having been assaulted by his live-in-partner-lady-rabbit Billie.

69

Read Chris Pascoe's column every week!

Short stories, health experts, interviews, great recipes, fashion and beauty buys

On Sale Every Tuesday

Domestic violence in the rabbit community is an often overlooked problem.

Because of Ted's habits of winding Billie up (usually by eating her furniture or sleeping in her food), falling through holes, rolling down stairs and jumping head first at solid objects, it's always been impossible to judge exactly how long he has left in him.

I've never given him more than a couple of weeks. Maximum. But this week, after an unexpected complication following his aforementioned operation, I thought he was finally on his way to join El-Ahrairah in the great warren in the sky. (Note to self: referencing *Watership Down* in a non-rabbit-based national magazine is an idiotic thing to do.)

One moment Ted seemed perfectly OK, the next he took ill in dramatic style. No half measures with this lad; he simply looked at us in what appeared to be total surprise, then fainted and tumbled

The cost would be high, survival chances slim, but this was Ted

off the top shelf of his hutch.

We rushed him straight to the vet, who grudgingly admitted there may still be a chance for him. We were advised though, that the cost would be high and survival chances slim. But this was Ted; we couldn't write him off over a thing like money, even if the final cost was nearly £700. (Yes, £700!)

After two days on a drip, being pumped full of all sorts of drugs, he suddenly sat up and resumed scratching as if nothing had happened, but £700 had certainly happened.

I've told him he'd better not pull a stunt like that again, but you'll certainly know about it if he does – just watch this space for my crowd-funding plea.

Telling
TAILS!

We take a short 'paws' to chat to our entertaining columnist, Chris Pascoe

Chris is a busy man, combining family life around his professional cat-sitting job, his writing career, occasional work as a mystery shopper and until recently, employment at a call centre, too.

"I was originally the manager of a courier delivery company but at the time when my daughter Maya came along in 2000, my wife Lorraine was earning much more than me,"

Wife Lorraine and daughter Maya

explains Chris, as he attempts to gently prize away a kitten which has decided to mountaineer up his back. "My salary barely covered the cost of Maya's nursery, so I packed it in to look after her. It was then that I started writing properly too. I had always done a little bit of writing, I'd even had some pieces published in My Weekly, but while Maya was sleeping I wrote my first book A *Cat Called Birmingham*."

"It was actually due to Brum (Birmingham's nickname) that the cat sitting started. Brum was banned from a local cattery, having howled the whole place down one weekend. We reasoned that if he was that stressed, others might feel the

A cuddle from Chris
for anti-hero Ted

73

same. We were the first cat sitters in our area, just doing the occasional visit but now it's a full time job. There is another car sitter nearby now, so we look after hers when she is away and vice versa. I write while I'm sitting with cats."

"At home we have our own cats Bodmin, Jojo ('the haughty-tortie') and Spooky. Bodmin turned up about three years ago. He came through the cat flap and just collapsed, in a terrible state. He stank because of an abscess, he had no fur on his head because of harvest mites and his gums had receded so he had fangs. We rushed him to the vets to get him sorted out and he's been with us ever since."

Rabbits Ted and Billie add to the menagerie that continues to provide a rich seam of material for Chris to plunder for his weekly column.

"I have always had good observational skills and I can glean inspiration from as little as one comment in a conversation. I email ideas to myself from my phone, even if they come to me when I wake in the night. I have

Billie and Ted

Spooky out exploring

Jojo, the "haughty Tortie"

Bruiser Bodmin

most ideas when I'm driving between cat visits, which is annoying because then I have to pull over to email myself. When I'm on a visit and the cats are playing around me I'll just open the emails and start writing part of an article on my phone or on my tablet, then add to the text on the next visit. So a lot of my articles get written over the course of the day at cat visits."

Chris's family often find themselves in print, too.

"My Dad gets a right panning but he loves it really and I think the family actually quite enjoy it too. My teenager Maya doesn't mind although she does insist on vetting anything that mentions her. I prefer writing my columns to books by far and I really love writing for My Weekly. It's a breath of fresh air to be able to write about all sorts of different subjects."

And with that, Chris is off to make one last 'catcall' before rushing off to a family wedding. Perhaps we'll be reading about it soon!

Don't miss Chris's column every week in My Weekly

Chris's Animal Magic

Chris has three cats of his own and, of course, he encounters many felines on his daily cat-sitting rounds. But it's not just cats who lead Chris on a merry dance. Seagulls, geese, monkeys, swans and even wallabies take their toll on this hapless animal lover.

WHAT'S IN A NAME?

It's not the imposing Boris but the dainty Pixie who causes most damage…

A customer called me this week, to give me a quick update on her cat Boris's circumstances ahead of her forthcoming holiday.

Boris is a Persian, named for his likeness to the previous Mayor of London. It's not only because of his great mop of golden hair, but also an eagerness to be present at every Opening available – as long as the opening involves a tin of cat food.

Boris had always been an indoor cat.

"Hi Chris, just a couple of changes. We've finally smashed a hole in the wall and Boris has a catflap now."

"OK, that's good – so how's he taking to the great outdoors?"

"Not too bad – we've got a bit of a problem with him chasing the birds, but otherwise fine."

The Mayor of London immediately sprang back to mind, but I thought it best not to comment.

"Oh – and one other thing, Chris. We've done away with his litter tray – hope that's OK with you?"

"I've never missed a litter tray yet!" I blurted out, instantly regretting my wording – this was clearly a statement that could be taken in very much the wrong way.

Fortunately, Mrs Johnson (not really her name!) didn't pick up on it. But I'm not always the greatest at choosing the right words

– which was never more evident than during a recent visit to the doctors, made on account of wounds suffered in the line of my cat-sitting duties.

"More wounds? What's the matter with you?" I can almost hear you asking. "Only last week that rat almost took your nose off, didn't it!" Well true, it's not been a good run – the rat Dirty Harry is still gnawing at my gloves on a daily basis.

However it was a Cornish Rex cat named Pixie, with legs as thin as a pencil and standing only seven inches tall in her white-paw-socks, who broke my toe.

Pixie is so tiny that there's absolutely no way she can go outside, despite her pleading smiles (she has a constant expression that would put the Cheshire Cat to shame). In fact, she made a dramatic run for the front door as I opened it one morning.

"We've a bit of a problem with him chasing the birds…"

My instinct was to swiftly block her route with my right foot. This deft little manoeuvre only almost worked. The resulting loud crack and blinding pain told me that my foot had not fared well.

On the plus side, the noise stopped Pixie dead in her tracks. For the briefest of moments, I'm sure that pixie smile of hers became an elfish laugh.

Anyway, when I hobbled in to see the nurse, on account of my little toe suddenly looking larger than my big one, I'm not sure how I could have explained that I thought I'd broken my toe any less clearly than I did.

"Just leave it alone," mumbled the nurse. "It'll fall off after a while."

It was probably the look of total horror on my face that prompted her to offer to take a look anyway,

"Ah, your toe! Thought we were talking toenails!"

You go in for a broken toe, they give you a coronary… 🐾

ANOTHER FINE MESS!

The cat-sitter is caught up in some painful feline slapstick…

You could be forgiven for thinking that cat-sitting is quite a "nice" job.

Well, it might be 90% litter tray-scooping, sick-sponging, faeces clearance and rodent-corpse disposal, but it's not all glamour.

On the glamour front though, I've just taken on two new cat clients named Stan and Ollie, and is there any pair of names more famous than that? You'd take a guess on them being a bit of a double act, wouldn't you?

In fact, there was indeed comedy and it did involve a double act. Unfortunately the double act was me and Stan.

The action began as I prepared the duo's breakfast. Their food bowls are kept on a wooden tray, and I'd placed the tray on the kitchen work-surface to dish up dinner and change the water. With the job complete, I pulled the tray towards me – just as Stan jumped up to the work-surface to find out what was taking me so long.

He hit the bottom of that tray like a ginger torpedo. He bounced backwards off the tray, returning to the ground with a backside-first thump, only to be hit by a cat-food hailstorm and a pint of cold water.

He took it very well – slicing my ankle in three places and ripping my sock. It was a Garfield sock as well. For the next minute or two he was a wildcat, ears back, soaked fur bristling, growling and stalking. I decided to leave him be and headed for the first-aid box.

As I left the room I noticed Ollie watching us. He had a kind of

resigned look, as if this was the sort of thing he saw happen to Stan every day.

Five minutes later Stan was as right as rain, and I was refilling bowls. He jumped up onto the work-surface and brushed his face against my arm as I placed a waterbowl under the tap. I smiled – all was well again.

I'm not quite sure how I managed to turn the tap on full blast into a tiny round metal bowl. The resulting 100 mile per hour splashback hit Stan full-on – for a moment I actually lost sight of his face in a huge deluge of white water, and then he was gone… flying back to the floor absolutely drenched from ear to tail. He was livid. Absolutely spitting feathers…and socks.

Ollie stared bemusedly as I headed out for further treatment.

A little while later, as a still soaked Stan sat purring on my lap

Ollie stared, bemused, as I headed off for more first aid

and ensuring everybody I met in the next half hour would assume I'd wet myself, I remembered where I'd seen that look (Ollie's look, not the wet-trouser-look). It was the very same look that the original Ollie used to give Stan in countless old black and white movies.

Thinking back now, and piecing together Ollie's look and Stan's chaotic comedy kitchen capers, I wonder whether I've been looking after just any old Stan and Ollie, or the real thing. Laurel & Hardy, reincarnated… as two ginger toms!

We certainly get to meet the stars, we cat-sitters.

GO WILD WITH BRYAN FERAL!

Our holiday chalet's charming visitor had a dark side… and mean friends

I've just spent a few days at a holiday village in a lovely forest setting beside a lake. Three days away from cat sitting didn't change things very much – I arrived home absolutely covered in cat scratches.

The culprit had appeared at our holiday chalet within minutes of our arrival. He was wonderfully friendly from the word go, brushing around our legs and standing up on his hind paws for strokes. After around two hours, it became very clear he had no intention of leaving.

I asked at reception about the cat and they explained that the village has a large feral cat community, living in the forest and attracted by a plentiful food supply. I've since discovered that it's estimated there are over a million feral cats living in the UK, and many of them form colonies in and around holiday locations such as ours.

How intelligent is that? Seeking out cat-lovers who are temporarily bereft of their furry friends smacks of total genius!

Anyway back to Bryan. Yes, that's right, we called our new chalet-mate Bryan. A long haired tabby with a strange mop of fur on the top of his head just had to be named after legendary Roxy Music frontman Bryan Ferry, or in this case…Bryan Feral.

Bryan Feral spent the entire three days at our chalet and became

85

a firm friend. He received food on demand, constant brushing, stroking and a nice, comfy, warm sofa to sleep on.

There was only one condition – the patio door had to be left open at all times. If we tried to shut it, panic set in. A panicky Bryan Feral wasn't nice at all, and the vivid red lines on my left arm are testament to this. But, as long as the door remained open a crack, Bryan was a happy cat.

On the last day, after much debate, we wondered if there was any way Bryan would come home with us, to start a new life in a cosy house with two new feline companions, a bright and beautiful rabbit…and Ted. After knowing us for three days, would he trust us to shut the door? And, if we got over that hurdle, was there any way he'd let us take him home? All very doubtful, but we thought we owed it to Bryan to give it a try.

Shirt ripped, I threw the patio doors open in a state of shock

Two minutes later, I threw the patio doors open in shock, my right arm now also covered in scratches, my shirt ripped and a bowl of cat food upside down on the carpet.

As I stepped outside in an attempt to calm the crazed Bryan, a swan hammer-beaked me straight in the groin.

A swan. Where the hell did that come from? I remember thinking as I sank to my knees. I wonder if there's anybody else in the world who's ever been attacked by a cat and a swan at the same time?

Bryan Feral stayed on vacation at the village. We're going back again soon, and we've booked the same chalet, very much hoping he'll still be there. If he is, we'll be welcoming him in with open arms again.

He can leave his flipping swan outside, though.

GETTING GOOSEBUMPS

It's not only cats that have it in for Chris – ducks and geese stalk him, too!

I've been having a few problems with ducks. In fact, not only ducks, but also their big cousins, geese.

The first attack came at a lovely riverside pub called, no, not The Drunken Duck, but the Red Lion.

While sitting with my wife Lorraine and daughter Maya, munching crisps and sipping shandy (I live a hell-raising existence) a large goose passing by on the river, stopped mid-swim and suddenly stared at me, as if stunned to see me there.

My daughter pointed this out, and we both laughed. This was a mistake – the goose seemed angered, as if he had the crazy idea I was laughing at him.

We watched with interest as said goose climbed out of the water, shook himself down, and waddled across the lawn towards us. After what seemed an age, he finally arrived at our table and stopped directly in front of me, staring coldly.

"Aww, he's lovely," said Lorraine. "He's come over to say hello!" Maya echoed the sentiment. I wasn't so sure.

I nodded hello and turned back to our table. The goose seemed affronted by this, and tapped me on the back with his beak. Maya and Lorraine laughed and crooned over how he just wanted a bit of attention, so I attempted a gentle stroke of his head.

This wasn't a good idea… his wings spread wide, he snapped

wildly at my hands and began honking for all he was worth. He was clearly completely livid.

I quickly turned back to the table, sipping my shandy and feigning nonchalance. This time it wasn't a gentle tap on the back, it was a sharp rap straight to the spine. As Maya got a faceful of shandy spray and Lorraine jumped from her seat, the crazed goose struck again and again…

Being chased into a pub by a goose is not a dignified way to enter any licensed premises. However, as I slammed the door shut behind me, noting surprised expressions all around, I decided that humiliation had been the better option.

This wasn't to be the end of my river-bird problems. While researching an English Civil War battle with my only-here-for-the-beer fellow researcher Pete, we tried to enter

He snapped **wildly** at my hands, honking for all he was **worth**

another pub via a small wooden footbridge over a narrow stream.

I suddenly became aware of a multitude of ducks spilling out over the banks of the stream. It seemed more a scene from World War One than the English Civil War, as if some beaked Captain had blown his whistle and his duck troops were pouring "over the top".

Pete hardly seemed to notice them until he was engulfed to the knees in quacking ducks and desperately trying not to stand on any.

I think it was this conscientious objection to harming them that caused him to wobble dangerously, take two giant strides and then bunny hop sideways straight into the stream.

I'm not sure who looked the most demented – the shocked man standing in a foot of water, or the one on the bank, surrounded by ducks and laughing uncontrollably.

WHEN CATS GO BAD...

A couple of unbelievable headlines grabbed Chris's attention this week...

The other day I read a news story under the huge banner headline ZOMBIE CAT RETURNS FROM THE GRAVE.

As a catsitter with an overactive imagination this was not the type of headline I wanted to be reading. Also, although having suffered a long history of bites and gouges at the paws of our feline friends, I hadn't yet contemplated the possibility of one of my furry charges attempting to eat my brain!

However, it seems that the cat in question, a Florida-based black and white tom named Bart, probably wasn't dead when he turned up on his owner's doorstep and meowed to be let in.

The only complication here was that Bart had been run over three days previously and buried.

Rather than a zombie turning up on the doorstep then, it must have been a very annoyed cat indeed. Bad enough to get knocked unconscious by a car, but then to have your well-meaning owner bury you in the woods… that's really annoying.

A US animal expert has theorised that Bart probably regained consciousness underground, dug his way back to the surface and then made his way home.

Considering he'd been buried, and then arrived home covered in mud, I can't really see why an expert needed to explain this, but he did and so it's official.

The article didn't comment on the current state of relations between Bart and his owner, but I know very well what happens when you disrespect a cat, and burying one alive would be right up there on the disrespectful-behaviour ratings. I hope the owner has a good supply of sticky plasters.

Finishing the article and shaking my head in wonder, I noticed another headline listed under "Related Stories": POLICE ARREST FAMILY CAT AFTER TWO HOUR SIEGE.

Another misleading headline surely? But no. Apparently, after a minor scratching incident, the cat's owner, a Mr Palmer of Portland, Oregon gave him an admonishing slap. As in the previous story, the cat would no doubt have seen this as disrespectful and a fight broke out. According to Mr Palmer the cat then flew into a terrible rage.

Mr Palmer, his wife and baby, and even their dog, were all

"He's charging at our door!" a panicked voice told the operator

forced to shut themselves in a bedroom, while the furious cat repeatedly charged at the bedroom door whenever they tried to make a break for it.

After a long siege they were forced to call the police. The police telephone transcript is really quite wonderful:

"He's charging at us," a panicked Mr Palmer told the 911 operator. "He's at our door, bedroom door!"

"He's trying to attack us. He's very, very, very angry."

The operator instructed Mr Palmer to keep calm and wait for assistance.

"Tell them to be careful… the police…" said Mr Palmer.

Police officers finally arrived on the scene and captured the cat as he made a daring bid for freedom by jumping on top of the fridge.

American cats, eh? You can't live with 'em, you can't bury 'em…

CAUGHT IN A CAT TRAP!

Chris gets a holiday from cat attacks – and becomes a spectator instead

I often feel that, wherever I am in the world and even if I were disguised as a dog, a local cat would seek me out and demand to be cat-sat.

I should point out that I haven't been travelling the world disguised as a dog but I have just returned from the Canary Isles, where I became acquainted with the local cat population, most of whom seemed to live on our balcony.

It was an odd sight every morning, pulling back the curtains, letting the sub-tropical sunlight flood into the room, and instantly being confronted by around 15 expectant feline faces.

Of course, powerless to disobey those pointy-eared inscrutable stares, I fed them. Being on an all-inclusive holiday, I suppose it was inevitable that 95% of our overall expenditure was on cat food at the local supermarket.

Surprisingly, none of the cats scratched, bit, mauled or accidentally attempted to put me in hospital. Oh no, it was a German guest (whose name I later discovered was Tomas) who suffered at their paws.

I first noticed him when I was on our balcony late one evening. All was quiet around the hotel grounds when suddenly our Teutonic hero came staggering from the general direction of the hotel bar and swerved dangerously close to the pool before

95

stopping, sensibly steadying himself.

Suddenly, from nowhere, a black and white cat came speeding across his path and as he desperately attempted to step over it, a tabby came bolting after it at breakneck speed. Tomas didn't stand a chance. Already off balance and on one foot, he pirouetted sideways before crashing into a flowerbed. Then all was still again – there was only the moonlight, the gentle lapping of the pool and a German gent lying face-down in the flowers.

This wasn't his only brush with the feline population. One afternoon I stepped out onto our balcony and spotted him relaxing on a sun lounger by the pool. Lounging directly above his head on top of one the pool area's huge sun umbrellas lay one of his arch enemies… a cat.

What happened next was disaster-comedy of the highest order. The cat stretched luxuriantly in the sunshine, rolled onto his back and carried on rolling, straight off the umbrella onto Tomas's chest.

The cat stretched luxuriantly, rolled over and off the umbrella

In total shock, Tomas shot upwards and forwards, grabbing the cat as he went.

Ever seen one of those poolside sun-beds that tip up if you put all your weight on one end? Yes? Well, it was one of those. The bed flipped upright, catapulting both cat and Tomas into the pool, the cat thrashing wildly and removing sections of Tomas's skin.

The whole thing took on the appearance of a scene from Jaws. Panicking mothers hauled their children from the water, while man yelled and cat screeched. Finally the drenched cat clambered out, leaving Tomas standing neck-deep in a deserted pool, no doubt wondering what he'd ever done to cats to provoke such awful treatment.

MONKEY BUSINESS

Where can you go to get your car wrecked by hooligan baboons? Chris knows...

Regular readers of this column will know there is a recurring theme running through a number of my stories; a series of incidents concerning various members of the animal kingdom. Much of this may stem from the fact that I work with animals, come home to animals, even sometimes go on holiday with animals, so naturally there are always going to be incidents involving animals, but I was thinking this morning about something that happened long before I was involved in pet-care. It concerned baboons.

On the site that is now Legoland (where I once queued for two hours for a ride that wasn't working – there's a day of my life I'll never get back) there once stood a safari park. The park's main highlight was attempting to drive through the baboon enclosure without one of them defecating on your car bonnet.

So why, at the tender age of 18 and driving my mum's car, did I give in to my then girlfriend, a learner driver, and let her take the wheel and run the baboon gauntlet? Probably because she was stupid pretty and I was pretty stupid. Anyway, she coped well enough trundling through zebras and giraffes, but at the first sight of a troop of baboons running towards us, she screamed, froze in panic and… stopped the car.

"Drive on!" I shouted.

BUNNY 5

She began crying.

Within seconds we were totally engulfed in baboons. Five minutes later I was still trying to take control of the car, which was now disappearing piece by piece. I stared in horror as one ape slapped another with a windscreen wiper, only to receive a flying wing-mirror to the side of his head. This was not going well, for me or the baboons.

Then suddenly, we began moving. My girlfriend, seemingly gaining some inner strength from watching baboons beat the hell out of each other, was determinedly driving forward.

Straight into a tree.

I think the very worst thing about all this, aside from the attack and having to be rescued by armed park rangers, was trying to explain it all to my mother, as I hadn't actually asked permission to take her pride-and-joy Fiat into a safari park.

Ridiculously, I tried blaming all the damage on crashing into

Apes slapped each other with Mum's windscreen wipers

a tree. However, Mum "failed to understand" how hitting a tree could result in the loss of her windscreen wipers, indicator lenses, wing mirrors and door trims. The simian footprints all over the roof really gave it away.

I had to choose – either claim angry monkeys had fallen from the tree when I hit it and ripped the car apart, or come clean. She stared in amazement as I recounted the angry monkeys falling from the tree story.

After a moment's silence, she went ballistic. If you're reading this, Mum, in my defence, I only ever had one of your cars destroyed by marauding apes.

FAREWELL OLD FRIEND

Saying goodbye to his mischievous partner in crime was never going to be easy

As regular readers of my weekly column are probably aware, I have two books "out there", *A Cat Called Birmingham* & *You Can Take the Cat Out of Slough...* (plug plug) all about one particular long-haired tabby cat named Brum. He was not just any long-haired tabby cat but very probably the most accident-prone cat in the world.

The fact that not one, but two, complete books could be written about his misadventures goes some way to justifying this grand title.

Brum's list of achievements is commendable. This is a cat who set his own head on fire, fell twenty feet onto a moving car, blew up the household electrics and lost a year-long war with a sparrow. And he came out of it all without a scratch. Singed whiskers and a few sparrow pecks to the ears maybe, but no scratches.

I also have a book out about a year long tour of the English Civil War battlefields, but nobody believes I wrote that one, mainly because only two chapters out of twenty involve cats. My answer to that has to be... have you ever seen any other book on the English Civil War, any book on the subject at all, that devotes two entire chapters to cats? Exactly.

What other idiot would do something like it?

Anyway, I'm frequently asked by readers whether Brum is still with us, so I thought, for all those interested, and as my own little tribute to Brum, I'd answer the question.

Brum…

Sometimes you don't realise just how good a friend somebody is, until they're gone.

Brum left us on a cold February morning. My old sparring-partner was suddenly taken ill and rushed to the vets where it was rapidly decided his best option was to be put to sleep.

Not the greatest best option ever, but the kindest to him, and thus presenting me with one of the most galling decisions of my life.

I didn't want it to be that way. I wanted him to go naturally – although, to be fair, going naturally for Brum would have been in a serious accident, probably taking half a dozen people and a couple of buildings with him! But I didn't want to be the one to condemn him to his fate.

His eyes appeared relaxed and focused on some faraway place

To sign one normal, innocent-looking piece of paper meant consenting to the end of Brum's life. My signature meant goodbye.

Eventually I squiggled my name, my hands shaking and my throat dry.

Brum seemed someplace far away as they shaved a little patch into his fur, in readiness for the last of those accursed injections he'd hated all his life.

His eyes appeared relaxed, and focused on some faraway place, way beyond the grey and grim vet walls and the traffic that roared past outside – looking back, I like to think, to his favourite spot at the top of the garden, on a much happier, summer day.

Then, in his last moments, he looked up into my eyes and gently laid a paw on my hand. His eyes closed, and Brum's story was finally over. 🐾

SIZE REALLY MATTERS

There's no happy medium in this story of three cats and the battle of the food bowl

I received a letter from a reader recently – a lovely letter, full of charm and humour, but – there was always going to be a "but", wasn't there? – one thing puzzled the sender. She'd seen an old photo of me on a book cover and, having compared it to my current photo, noted an alarming discrepancy.

I'll take her next line to the grave with me: "I assume they must have stretched your photo to fit a certain space, since the proportions of height and width seem to have been reversed."

Now you tell me if there's any better way of telling someone they've piled on the weight, and I'd like to know about it.

So, on the very loose subject of big appetites, I thought I'd give a cat named Medium Dave a mention this week. They say that everyone has a friend called Dave. I have three, and they're all cats. Medium Dave was named after a Terry Pratchett character (the middle sized member of a group of Daves) and, in honour of the late great Terry, Dave's owner named his cats accordingly. How else could anyone end up with three cats named Dave?

Naming mistakes were clearly made though, because Medium Dave grew up to love food with a passion. At feeding time he's a manic wreck in anticipation of the gastronomical delights to come. He then becomes so happy when eating that he purrs, mews and chomps throughout his meal, giving the impression that he's

103

Medium Dave

Big Dave

Little Dave

104

singing a song with his mouth full. This doesn't last long as he demolishes his meal in 10 seconds flat, quickly turning his attention to his fellow Daves' food.

If I'm not quick enough to stop him, a flying leap will end with Big Dave and Little Dave's heads being shoved straight into their own bowls as he attempts to eat their meals through the backs of their heads. For this reason, his brothers are frantically fast eaters, too.

The overall food panic in the house is infectious. By the time we're moving on to the dry food main course, I'm often subconsciously moving at three times my normal speed (pretty fast for a fat lad) in a desperate bid to meet the Daves' crazed demands. So much so that I once opened a 1.5 kg bag of Purina in the style of the Incredible Hulk ripping off his shirt, causing a thousand small biscuits to explode in all directions.

This scatter-gun approach to cat feeding is not to be

The explosion of food has the cats bounding round the room

recommended. The sudden unexpected explosion of food had all three cats bounding around the room, pouncing on every ricocheting morsel, in what looked very much like a stampede of Daves.

Medium Dave could certainly do with going on a diet and, with my reader's email in mind, I'm beginning to think a diet is in order for me, too. I need to arrest my height and width reversal before it's too late. If I don't, then the next time my My Weekly pic is updated, I'll be needing an extra page or two.

FANCY THAT!

Animal facts to make you go "wow"

A group of geese is called a skein in flight, a gaggle on the ground, and a flock anywhere.

Around 75% of the species found on Madagascar live nowhere else on the planet.

Squirrels plant thousands of trees every year. They bury nuts then forget to dig them up again.

A group of kittens is called a kindle.

Eagles have such good eyesight, they can spot prey from a distance of two miles.

Sea otters hold hands while sleeping to prevent them from drifting apart.

The viral sensation Grumpy Cat has earned her owners millions in branded merchandise, endorsements and even her own movie.

Almost half the pigs in the world are kept by farmers in China.

Cows can sleep standing up but can only dream lying down.

Male cats are more likely to be left-pawed, while females are more likely to be right-pawed.

Wallabies and kangaroos are competent swimmers, adopting a sort of "doggy paddle" style.

The Norse goddess Freyja travels in a chariot pulled by two giant black stray cats.

Tigers not only have stripes on their fur, they have stripes on their skin. No two tigers have exactly the same stripes.

Sir Isaac Newton is credited with inventing the cat flap.

A LOVER OF MEW-SIC!

The haughty tortie delivered the harshest critique of all

Cat sitting is actually quite a lonely job. There's very little human contact – all the houses I visit are completely devoid of people.

They have to be this way of course, or there'd be no point in my visiting them.

So considering my average daily contact is almost entirely with cats, has my behaviour become more cat-like?

Of course not. Well, actually… maybe.

I'm not saying I now stalk sparrows for fun or carry small rodents around in my teeth (in my pocket, yes) but I do sometimes find myself meowing back at cats.

I also seem to have developed a cat-like patience that wasn't there before. I can happily sit for ages with a cat, just staring at a goldfish tank, or even a wall. A cat creates the atmosphere of total calm that enables me to do this.

Then, of course, for no apparent reason the cat will jump to sudden attentiveness with wide-eyed, fur-bristling shock, and I'll jump two feet off the chair.

So, to keep sane in my job, I tend to talk and sing quietly as I prepare meals and clean litter trays, just for the normality of human noise. Thinking about it, the fact I've just admitted to meowing at cats and regularly talking to myself may suggest that I'm not exactly succeeding on the "keeping sane" front.

One thing I've discovered, though, is that cats don't like my singing. These furry little Simon Cowells have made this very clear.

Poppy, for instance, a usually gentle and serene cat, took violent exception to my rendition of *Always Look on the Bright Side of Life*. I was washing her food bowl, singing away, when I noticed her staring with something approaching disbelief. Still singing, I gave the top of her head a little brush. She almost took my hand off.

Tilly, a slightly skittish but generally charming tabby, was so horrified by my *What's New Pussycat* that she bolted from the kitchen, so fast that her back legs skidded three times on the lino floor.

I stopped singing and she sidled warily back into the room, ears back, listening like a hawk for any sign of an encore.

Out of interest, I sang the same song to my own tortoiseshell, Jojo. At first, her reaction seemed calm – much better than my

Poppy took violent exception to my *Always Look On The Bright Side*...

previous audiences. Then she yawned, stretched, got up from her cat-bed, walked casually to our indoor clothes airer and, with a deft flick of claws, ripped my best T-shirt.

She then strutted from the room, head and tail in the air. The haughty tortie had delivered the harshest critique of all.

I mentioned all this to my wife, Lorraine.

"You sing?" she said. "To cats?" No, I explained, not to them, more at them really.

Not being familiar with my singing, as it's not something I do at home, she suggested I sing a couple of lines. Her verdict? I'm becoming more cat-like than even I'd realised.

THE HEIGHT OF STUPIDITY

Escaped indoor cat Leonard Cohen isn't the only one out of his comfort zone...

You could be forgiven for thinking that catsitting is quite a nice job. Well, it might be 90% sick-sponging and faeces disposal, but it's not all glamour.

I discovered the darker side of cat-sitting when looking after a cat named Leonard Cohen over the Christmas holidays. Leonard's a strictly indoor cat, but on arrival I found him to be, strictly speaking, outside.

Not just a little bit outside – more vanished-off-the-face- of- outside. A previously locked catflap hanging off its hinges gave me a clue as to how he'd achieved this.

For hours I searched the streets and checked with neighbours, but to no avail. I fixed Leonard's catflap, set it to incoming-only and hoped he'd come home.

He didn't, and continual searching yielded no trace. Desperately trawling the internet for ideas, I found plenty of advice. Apparently Leonard's behaviour was typical of escaped indoor cats who, once out, are often terror-stricken and retreat to a permanent hiding place.

A night search of bushes was advised, using a torch to catch the reflection of his eyes. I do everything websites tell me to do, so I returned that evening.

The first thing I found was that my incoming-catflap had worked

well. I'd trapped a cat … but not the right one. The snarling nightmare that greeted me in the kitchen was not Leonard, and not happy.

In fact, he was so not happy to see me, he lunged at a window in a desperate bid to escape, smashing teacups, upending pots and lacerating my hand. Things were going well.

Opening the door to release him and stumbling outside, I saw something that made my heart leap with joy. There, sitting on a low flat roof above the door, was Leonard Cohen.

Soothing words and skilful coaxing totally failed to get him down, so I climbed onto a patio chair and reached out slowly to him, crooning gently. At this moment, with the situation delicately poised, the chair decided I was too fat to be standing on it, and collapsed.

My face contorted in surprise and my head lurched forward. As I watched Leonard bound away across the rooftops, I realised my

The chair decided I was too fat to be standing on it and collapsed

ankle wasn't able to support me any longer, and so I fell over.

The story has a happy ending. Leonard obviously heard that I'd been admitted to A&E, and due to the normal backlog of injured seasonal revellers, had virtually no chance of coming out any time soon.

So he immediately returned home where my wife, who'd taken over the job, found him sleeping happily on the sofa.

I'd like to claim some credit for Leonard's safe return, but I can only be credited with smashed teacups, obliterated garden furniture, a swollen ankle and gashed hands.

The great thing is though, when you've ended the year as well as I have, the potential for personal improvement is breathtaking!

MISSION IMPLAUSIBLE

This latest job was going to take military precision and a careful step...

I've been visiting a couple of Royal Air Force rabbits over the past week. These rabbits are specially trained to burrow under enemy lines and, upon reaching their target, radio GPS coordinates to their RAF colleagues in the air, bringing down precision airstrikes… probably.

Actually, probably not – they just happen to belong to a Royal Air Force family and as far as I can see they just run around eating carrots all day.

This was the first time I've ever had to go "behind the wire" at the base, and it was a very interesting experience.

The gate was being guarded by a man dressed from head to toe in camouflage fatigues. On top of all this camouflage, he wore a hi-vis jacket. Now, is it just me, or isn't that a bit of a no-no. Hi-vis camouflage?

Beside the gate stands a full size replica Spitfire. Having just met the hi-vis guard, I looked at this plane in a new light. It too was camouflaged… but on its sides, wings and tail were great big bullseye targets.

I've always wondered how the RAF ever came to the alarming decision that it'd be a really great idea to paint targets all over their aircraft.

"Right, pay attention gentleman, it's time to decide on insignia

115

for our planes. Now remember, they'll be flying sorties over some of the world's most dangerous places, constantly dodging the fire of both anti-aircraft guns and enemy planes. Any ideas anyone?"

"Um, how about painting massive bullseye targets all over them?"

"Excellent suggestion, Bombardier, we'll go with that."

Inside the base is a sign instructing you to drive with your lights on. Presumably this is to ensure the base can be easily spotted by overhead enemy planes. What a sporting lot the RAF are.

Having cheerily waved to two hi-vis patrolmen, I arrived at the base's residential area and at the home of Victoria and Albert, the rabbits I'd be looking after.

Unlike most rabbits, this pair don't actually have a hutch. They live free inside the house, wandering around the lounge, kitchen, running up and down the stairs, and just basically doing whatever they choose, which turned out to be mainly running straight at my legs.

I arrived at the base's residential area and found Victoria & Albert

This was a major hazard for two reasons. Firstly, if you stand on a rabbit it's not like standing on a cat (it's bad that I know all this) which will just screech and take your toes off. A rabbit will break.

Secondly, in my desperate efforts to avoid standing on the two lop-eared lunatics criss- crossing my path, I managed to spill a full litter tray (yes, they even have a litter tray!) all over the hall carpet.

So, this week I've managed to stain a carpet belonging
to a man with a heavily armed fighter plane and probably trained to kill with his bare hands.

I'll most definitely be keeping an eye out for any clandestine hi-vis activity in the woods behind my house! 🐾

LED ASTRAY BY A MONKEY

There's a bit of monkey business going on with Chris this week

I'm currently looking after a cat named Monkey. Aside from Monkey probably living his life slightly confused as to why everyone constantly refers to him as an entirely different species, he's also no doubt highly perplexed as to why I'm looking after him at all. And so am I.

You see, jet black beautifully-coated Monkey lives in a house full of young people, who haven't actually gone anywhere. This is a first for me; the main point of my catsitting job being to feed cats while their humans are away, not while their humans are sitting eating their lunch in the same room.

This odd situation came about because Monkey's owners didn't mention, when booking me to cover their holiday, that they had two lodgers. Or that these two lodgers would have live-in boyfriends.

The visits began well though – Monkey is a friendly lad, he can spend over an hour just brushing his furry little face against my hands and legs, rolling over on his back, purring like a pneumatic drill. His only slightly odd trait is that he insists all this happens under the dining room table. He'll lead me there every visit, meow-shouting over his shoulder for me to follow. This I do, of course… I do everything shouting cats tell me to do.

It was while I was under the dining room table with Monkey that

Lodger One and her boyfriend suddenly entered the room with a takeaway meal and, with a cheery hello, sat down at the table and started eating.

"Hi," I replied, a little taken aback. "Sorry, I'll get out of your way and…"

"No no, you carry on, it's fine" said Lodger One.

"No really, I don't think –"

"Hey, it's okay, carry on, I can see Monkey's happy."

Oh no. She'd played the "think of the cat" card. Now I had no choice. Thus followed the most bizarre situation of my catsitting life (and I've had a few).

While a couple sat eating lunch and chatting happily to one another, I sat hunched under their table stroking a cat. Just when I thought things couldn't get any more embarrassing, Lodger Two walked into the room. She stopped dead in her tracks. Was the weird cat guy really sitting under her friends' table? Did they know

Thus followed the most bizarre situation of my catsitting life

he was there? I did all I could do in the circumstances – gave a big grin and raised my hand in a friendly wave.

Her return smile was about as forced as a smile could be, then she turned on her heel and left the room without a word, and she's been mainly ignoring me ever since.

I'm a catsitting spectre that flits round her house in the company of Monkey the cat and hides under tables when people are eating.

My reputation just gets better and better, doesn't it?

I'm still visiting Monkey, but the moment I hear anyone move in the house, he's in my arms and I'm out from under that table in a flash. I'm not getting caught like that again. 🐾

MAKING A BIG SPLASH

Chris, daughter Maya and a soggy moggy "enjoy" a hot summer...

The recent sunshine has reminded me of my days as a stay-at-home-toddler-sitter, and one summer in particular. As that summer got under way, it became patently clear that there was something wrong with it. It was the sun. It kept staying out. And as long as the sun stayed out, so too did Maya's paddling-pool; something she regarded as strictly private property.

I was never allowed in it, and Brum the cat was most definitely, absolutely, certainly not allowed in it. The slightest nose twitching curiosity was always met with a toddler-tantrum of terrifying force.

In the light of this you'd think Brum would've actively avoided diving headfirst into the thing, wouldn't you? But no, not Brum.

Never did a garden item provide so much wet calamity.

Four times in the first few weeks of summer I watched him swimming around, albeit extremely unhappily, totally drenched within its walls.

On one occasion he squelched into the lounge, obviously after an unobserved dip and immediately began sidling around Maya. As his wet fur slid along her legs, she tried to dodge sideways, shrieking with her hands in the air, but he slinked along with her. She tried to back up, but he went with her, always rubbing his soaked fur against her legs as she waved her hands frantically and screamed louder.

The scene became reminiscent of a dramatic Spanish dance, the pair striding around the room in perfect unison, her hands appearing to play invisible castanets as she wailed her tragic story and Brum looking deadly serious, head held proudly in the air.

Brum's range of pool splashdown approaches were varied and impressive, but I think for sheer surprise value, his catflap-superloop stood out as something quite special.

Brum had a "raging bull" approach to catflapping. After initial early life failures to get through it at all, he at some point decided that the only way was to ram it headfirst at 100mph.

I suppose, with hindsight, filling the pool right outside the catflap wasn't a great idea, but that's where the garden tap was – I had every intention of dragging it away afterwards.

And so it was that, as Maya and I watched the pool fill, her a demented mix of impatience and excitement, out of nowhere a determined- faced cat hurtled headlong at the pool, hit the rim,

Brum did a spectacular mid-air flip and sank beneath the waves

did a spectacular mid-air flip and sank beneath the waves with an almighty splash.

For the briefest of moments, only his four legs protruded from the water as his back hit the bottom.

Maya and I stood in silence, our jaws dropping in unison, before Maya suddenly gave a roar of sheer undiluted rage, angrily kicking and punching the air as I held her back. How dare Brum get in the pool before her!

Brum surfaced and glared at me – he instinctively knew I was to blame. Of course I was.

A few minutes later, unbelievably, Brum was back in the pool again, having been put there by an eagle. Well, sort of, and by almost an eagle. Read on to discover what on earth I'm going on about...

122

THE EAGLE HAS LANDED

Brum takes to the water in terror to escape the clutches of a new visitor...

L ast time, I talked about my cat Brum's penchant for falling in paddling pools… more specifically my then toddler Maya's paddling pool, something she guarded with uncompromising force.

Well, immediately after the unintended dip in the pool mentioned last week, Brum sloped off up our garden steps leaving a rather comical trail of wet paw-prints. As he reached the top of the garden, fifteen feet above me owing to the fact we live on something akin to the side of a mountain, he looked back, dripping menacingly.

I thought for one terrible moment he was about to perform a mountain-lion-pounce-and-kill, so annoyed did he look. Instead he gave a meek meow and lay down to dry out in the sunshine.

A couple of minutes later, unbelievably, he was back in the pool – so blinded by fear that it was a case of the pool being a better option.

The cause of Brum's terror? Something had just landed up there on the wall with him, something so unexpectedly terrifying that Brum actually shrieked as he ran full pelt down the garden steps and skidded round the corner.

Still looking over his shoulder, he hit the pool's plastic wall at breakneck speed, briefly collapsed it, and stumbled face first back

into the water. My initial disbelieving laughter stuck in my throat when I saw what he was running from.

As Brum thrashed around, gulping in huge mouthfuls of pool water and mainly trying not to die, I stared aghast at the eagle sitting in my garden. It stared back evilly, as eagles do, with unblinking eyes.

Brum, meanwhile, finally found his feet but didn't even attempt to leave the pool, deciding instead to stand stock still and join in all the staring. A sudden crescendo of pool bubbles confirmed that he was every bit as edgy as I was.

And so a standoff ensued – a huge eagle at the top of the garden, a man and a flatulent cat half-submerged in a paddling pool at the bottom.

At this point, Maya arrived back from a toilet break, her brow furrowing as she spotted Brum back in her pool. Oh no!

Sudden screams of toddler outrage broke the tense silence,

Seeing what he was running from my laughter stuck in my throat

causing a startled eagle to spread its truly enormous pair of wings and fly straight at us.

Brum ducked beneath the water and I grabbed Maya. As the eagle swooped, I fully expected Brum to be plucked from the pool like a scumrabbit. Instead the eagle gained height and soared away over the rooftops. Suspending disbelief, I ran indoors to alert the authorities.

Can you believe it? An eagle? In High Wycombe?

Well no, as it turned out, but nobody had told me red kite hawks had recently been released into the Chiltern Hills, so when a vicious-beaked, two-feet-tall bird with a six-foot wingspan suddenly lands in your garden, you're going to think it's an eagle, aren't you?

Well, I did, and I don't think that was so silly. The local police did, though. 🐾

SEAGULLS 4 CHRIS 0

Chris's encounters with seabirds make the cats, rats and rabbits look benign!

As regular readers know, I've had quite a few run-ins with members of the animal kingdom. I've been conned and outwitted by a caged rat, used as a pin cushion by various bloodthirsty cats, swooped at by an eagle, and knocked out by a rabbit. But last week, I met the big daddies of all animal assailants – seagulls.

It all kicked off on Brighton Pier, but at first I quite liked the resident hordes of marauding seagulls, and watching their constant daring dives for people's chips was actually making my day.

However, as I sat eating some noodles, watching all the general chip pilfering going on around me and chuckling quietly to myself, there was a sudden whoosh of wings and a squawk – and then noodles literally exploded in my hand.

They flew everywhere, but mostly down my shirt and trousers, chilli sauce and all. I sat aghast as the seagull whooshed happily away and a man holding chips laughed mercilessly at me.

A little while later, while still complaining bitterly to Lorraine about the unfairness of it all, a seagull swooped in for a grab at her ice cream, totally missed, and thudded straight into my face. Lorraine contemplated my rapidly bruising eye as she slurped thoughtfully on her Cornetto, before handing it to me for a conciliatory lick. No sooner had I taken it than the seagull was back

127

in for another try. I swear this gull needed a trip to Specsavers. He completely missed the ice cream once again, instead taking a huge peck out of my thumb. As I jumped around in agony, Lorraine glared. When you lend someone an ice cream, you don't expect to get it back covered in blood

This was great. I'd been on Brighton Pier 10 minutes and I looked like I'd gone 10 rounds with Mike Tyson. My shirt was covered in bright red chilli sauce, my left eye was swollen and my right hand was swathed in blood-stained tissues.

To emphasise how bad I looked, a little while later as I stood waiting for Lorraine outside a souvenir shop, a kindly old lady gave me 50 pence. That's how bad I looked.

Lorraine decided I could probably do with a drink, and there was no way I was arguing with her. So we sat down with beers at the wonderful Victoria Bar on Brighton

There was a squawk and then noodles exploded in my hand

Pier – a pub with a panoramic sea view from just about every table, indoor or out. We chose outdoor, so you can probably guess what was coming next…

After nipping inside for a quick trip to the powder room, Lorraine returned to find me slumped over my pint, head in tissue-wrapped hands, as a seagull sat beside me happily eating my crisps without a care in the world. I'd been utterly vanquished. The animal world had dealt me my greatest blow.

Watch out all you cats, rats and rabbits, when I get back to work on Monday I'll be giving you all extra strokes and treats – just as a thank you for not being seagulls.

STARS IN THEIR EYES

It's Monkey World, as seen on TV – but as usual Chris's mind is elsewhere

I went to Monkey World last weekend. I realise there are many who feel this is where I should have been all along, but it was actually my first visit.

For those who don't know, Monkey World is a primate rescue centre in Dorset which has achieved fame through a long-running reality TV series. The series follows the day-to-day life of both apes and staff, and so they've all become stars in their own right. My wife Lorraine loves it, mainly because she's a massive fan of primates – especially massive primates, which is probably the reason I stood a chance with her.

To acknowledge this, and in a "meet the family" type gesture, for her Christmas present I purchased tickets to Monkey World.

From the moment we walked through the theme park-style gates, Lorraine became more energised than I've ever seen her – something which may say as much about living with me as it does about Monkey World.

I watched incredulously as she ran from enclosure to enclosure, almost beside herself with excitement. Lorraine never runs, anywhere.

One moment she'd be pointing at a grinning chimpanzee shouting, "It's Bart, it's Bart! I can't believe it's Bart", the next she'd be shouting "Tau, Tau, look over this way!" at a tiny Capuchin

monkey, instantly recognising him despite the fact he was sitting among 23 almost identical compatriots.

Amazingly, it was indeed Tau. He looked round at Lorraine with an element of monkey-surprise, as if to say "Who, me?" To Tau's credit he then walked to our edge of the enclosure and tipped his wig to us. Have you ever seen a Capuchin monkey?

They have a mop of dark hair on the tops of their heads, and when they communicate (usually by raising their eyebrows) the whole lot seems to move up and down like a poorly-fitted toupée.

A little later, as a star-struck Lorraine met idol after idol, dashing from orangutans to chimps, from marmosets to gibbons and back to orangutans, I received a call on my mobile from a customer enquiring about my cat-sitting service.

"Can you tell me a bit about the business?" she asked.

"Certainly," I replied. "We've been established for 15 years and I'm an out-and-out cat lover. Apart from the cat-sitting, I write

Tau came over to the edge of the enclosure and tipped his wig

books about cats, and magazine columns about cats, and…"

"So you're very much a cat person then?"

"Oh yes," I laughed. "It's just cats, cats and more cats, nothing but cats."

At this moment I noticed a group of people stop in their tracks and stare at me in confusion. Why was this man shouting "Cats, cats and more cats" while gazing into a cage full of monkeys, with more monkeys as far as the eye could see… in Monkey World?

So, even in a park full of crazy, jumping, marauding apes, I still managed to come across as completely insane. Welcome to Pascoeworld. 🐾

SUCH MEAN MARSUPIALS

A wallaby in disguise is Chris's latest adversary from the animal kingdom

Given how often I write about a certain rabbit in My Weekly, you'd think by now I'd be able to recognise one, wouldn't you?

But no, on a recent family outing to Whipsnade Zoo, and after watching a herd of some sort of weird African deer not gliding majestically over the Savannah, but standing stock still in a rain-soaked field, I happened to notice a rabbit standing a few feet behind them. As I studied the rabbit, I noticed something not quite right about it.

"That's a really big rabbit," I suddenly exclaimed, causing my daughter Maya to spill hot chocolate down her front. "It can't be a rabbit, surely, it must be a hare?" I continued. "No, no, it's definitely a rabbit – an absolutely huge rabbit!"

An extremely irritated and chocolate-coated Maya wrenched the binoculars from my hands, a move which, considering I had them strapped around my neck at the time, had me hurtling sideways towards her.

Maya studied the rabbit for a few seconds, the top of my head trapped at a 45-degree angle against her cheek, and finally gave out a huge exasperated sigh.

"It's a wallaby! How on earth could you think a wallaby was a rabbit?"

133

Indeed. Humiliated by a wallaby then, and believe it or not, not for the first time. I have history with wallabies (that's a sentence you probably won't hear often). My Whipsnade wallaby woes go back 40 years, in fact.

On a forced school trip to the zoo in 1976, a free range wallaby stole my bag. As I sat on a hill, about to eat lunch, the bouncing marsupial appeared from nowhere, grabbed my bag and hopped off downhill at top speed.

Quarter of an hour it took me to get it back, running back and forth across a muddy field in front of 30 jeering classmates. I did finally recover it, but only because the vindictive animal finally decided to drop it into a pile of muck so copious I'm guessing the elephants had been out for a morning stroll.

Add to all that, a wallaby I tripped over in Coombe Martin, Devon a few years ago and it's quite a picture, isn't it? What was a wallaby even doing in a Devon Dinosaur theme park anyway?

How on earth could you think a wallaby was a rabbit?

I was looking up at Brachiosaurs and the like, not down… at wallabies.

Another thing about that particular theme park that baffles me to this day, is why they felt the need to have their animatronic dinosaurs double as slightly unsavoury impromptu water features. Still rubbing my knees after my wallaby incident, I stopped to admire a magnificent Tyrannosaurus, and it spat straight in my face. What an all-round lovely day that was.

And the moral of this story? Always remember rabbits are better than wallabies, and never trust a dinosaur from Devon.

Well, any advice from me was never going to be particularly useful, was it?

TAKING A QUICK DIP!

Walking a paranoid cat on a harness can only lead to disaster...

No, no," I stressed to my slightly annoyed catsitting client on the phone. "I'm certainly not saying Edcase is a nasty cat. I'm just saying he can be a bit feisty at times (read 'violently psychotic') and trying to take him for a walk might prove…problematic."

My client wouldn't be swayed, however. She often took Edcase for a walk on his harness, she told me, and he was fine about it. She also pointed out that he was never "feisty" with anyone else.

"OK," I conceded, wondering how Edcase came about his name if he really was all sweetness and light, "I'll definitely give it another try. It's just last time he gave me a bit of a nip (viciously imprinted his dental records on my forearm) but if you say he's fine now…"

It all started well. Edcase allowed me to fasten his harness with nothing but an interested meow, before being happily led into the garden for his morning constitutional. So happy was he, he skipped ahead of me, and it was at this point my problems began.

As Edcase walked on, he suddenly became aware that somebody was following him. Me. He stopped dead in his tracks and looked suspiciously over his shoulder. I stopped too. Edcase took another couple of steps, and so did I – I had to. Edcase was now almost certain he was being followed. He tried another couple of steps and, his suspicions confirmed, swung round and hissed.

135

Then, totally unexpectedly, he ran full pelt down the garden steps. Caught unawares and teetering dangerously on the top step, I had no choice but to go with him, running at breakneck speed down 15 steps before finally managing to bring myself to a halt just short of a fishpond.

The main problem with my sudden halt was that Edcase hadn't stopped, and instead attempted to vault over the pond and away from me.

There could be only one outcome. His leash twanged tight and he dropped like a stone straight into the middle of the pond.

Now I was in big trouble. As I desperately tried to help Edcase

I desperately tried to help Edcase out. He desperately tried to kill me

out of the water, Edcase desperately tried to kill me. When he finally did manage to clamber onto dry land, his next move was to take a sudden bolt to the right, draping his lead around an ornamental cat statue, causing me to send it splashing into the pond.

As I watched the statue's face sink slowly out of sight, I couldn't help but feel things weren't going that well. Two cats in a pond in two minutes – that's a record even for me.

After a lot of pulling and begging, I finally managed to get an absolutely livid Edcase back into his kitchen.

I won't go into too much detail about my efforts to remove the harness. Suffice to say that I did, and Edcase was soon happily purring again while I hunted for some plasters.

Cats hunt me, I hunt plasters. It's what we do.

My Weekly Pocket Novels

For women who love great stories

- Handy hand-bag size
- Full of drama and romance

138

My Weekly Specials

EXTRA!

Bumper puzzle mag inside

My Weekly Puzzle Bonanza
24
And LOTS More

My Weekly
special

£3.99

HOLIDAY READING

The Wadhams **ARE BACK!**

Cheese-tastic!

Best Ever **Cheese Meals!**

MENOPAUSE
We tell it like it **REALLY is!**

Dawn French
"Home is for happiness"

#31

Easy reading short stories & best summer crime novels

Nature's BEAUTY
At home and abroad

DR

On Sale Every Month

Competitions and offers open to UK residents only, unless otherwise stated

Great fiction, mind-stretching puzzles, health and wellbeing

ORDER FORM

Please complete the coupon below and send it to: My Weekly Subscriptions,
DC Thomson Shop, PO Box 766, Haywards Heath, RH16 9GF

YES, I would like to subscribe to **My Weekly** for:

❏ **BEST DEAL!** Only £4 for the first 3 months and £12 per quarter thereafter (UK) by direct debit*

❏ 1 year for £51.74 (UK) or £84.60 (Overseas) by cheque or credit/debit card

❏ 2 years for £98.30 (UK) or £160.74 (Overseas) by cheque or credit/debit card

Your Details

Title .... Name.. Address ....

....Postcode ....

Telephone..Email ....

Delivery Details (If different from above)

Title .... Name..Address ....

....Postcode ....

Telephone...

DIRECT DEBIT

DIRECT Debit

INSTRUCTIONS TO YOUR BANK/BUILDING SOCIETY TO
PAY BY DIRECT DEBIT

Originator's Identification Number

3	8	8	5	5	2

Name and full postal address of your Bank or Building Society

To the Manager	Bank/Building Society
Address	
	Postcode

Instruction to your Bank or Building Society
Please pay DC Thomson & Co Ltd Direct debit from the account detailed in this instruction subject to the safeguards assured by the Direct Debit Guarantee. I understand that this instruction may remain with DC Thomson & Co Ltd and if so, details will be passed electronically to my Bank/Building society.

Signature(s)

Name(s) of A/c Holder(s)

Date

Bank/Building Account No

FOR DC THOMSON & CO LTD OFFICIAL USE ONLY
This is not part of the instruction to your Bank or Building society.

Branch Sort Code

Bank and Building Societies may not accept
Direct Debits for some types of account

From time to time, DC Thomson & Co Ltd, Its group companies and partner businesses would like to contact customers to manage their account, for market research purposes and about new products, services and offers that we think will be of interest. We'll assume that DC Thomson & Co Ltd, Its group companies and partner businesses can contact you by email, post or telephone unless you tick the relevant box No contact from DC Thomson & Co Ltd or It's group companies unless It relates to an existing order ❏ No contact from our partner businesses ❏

My Weekly

FANTASTIC SUBSCRIPTION SAVINGS

SAVE OVER £56

SAVE OVER £20

My Weekly Pocket Novels
FIRST 6 ISSUES ONLY £2.50
£10.50 per quarter thereafter
One year price: £34

My Weekly Specials
FIRST 3 ISSUES ONLY £3
£8 per quarter thereafter
One year price: £27

GREAT REASONS TO SUBSCRIBE...

- **SAVE UP TO £56** WHEN PAYING BY DIRECT DEBIT.*
- **FREE UK DELIVERY** DIRECT TO YOUR DOOR.
- **GUARANTEED** TO RECEIVE YOUR COPY BEFORE IT'S IN THE SHOPS.
- **NEVER MISS** ANOTHER COPY OF YOUR FAVOURITE MAGAZINE.
- **QUALIFY** FOR EXCLUSIVE SUBSCRIBER DISCOUNT OFFERS.

DIGITAL SUBSCRIPTION NOW AVAILABLE ON PC, TABLET OR SMARTPHONE
Find out more at: **www.dcthomsonshop.co.uk/digital**

IT'S EASY TO ORDER!

FREEPHONE: **0800 318 846** quoting **MWPAS**.
(UK landlines and mobiles) 8am-6pm Mon-Fri, 9am-5pm Sat

ONLINE: **www.dcthomsonshop.co.uk/MWPAS**

Byron's WOMEN

Alexander Larman is a historian and journalist. He is the author of *Blazing Star* (2014), the life of Lord Rochester, and *Restoration* (2016), and writes for the *Observer*, the *Telegraph* and the *Guardian*, as well as the *New Statesman* and the *Times Literary Supplement*.